Powerful Kids

Shah Rukh

Published by Shah Rukh, 2024.

While every precaution has been taken in the preparation of this book, the publisher assumes no responsibility for errors or omissions, or for damages resulting from the use of the information contained herein.

POWERFUL KIDS

First edition. May 17, 2024.

Written by Shah Rukh.

Table of Contents

Introduction

In every generation, there are extraordinary young individuals who defy expectations, break barriers, and create transformative change. These are the powerful kids—youth who channel their energy, passion, and creativity into making a significant impact on their communities and the world at large. Their stories are not only a testament to their remarkable abilities but also a source of inspiration for others, proving that age is not a barrier to effecting meaningful change.

This book, "Powerful Kids," chronicles the lives and achievements of some of the most influential young changemakers of our time. From science prodigies and social entrepreneurs to activists and advocates, these young people have tackled some of the most pressing issues of our day, including education, climate change, health, and social justice. Through their stories, we gain insight into their motivations, challenges, and the incredible journeys that have shaped their paths to success.

In the chapters that follow, you will meet individuals like Malala Yousafzai, who stood up against the Taliban for her right to education and became a global symbol of courage and women's rights. You'll learn about Greta Thunberg, whose solo protests against climate change ignited a worldwide movement, and Jack Andraka, whose groundbreaking cancer research has the potential to save countless lives. These young people, along with many others featured in this book, demonstrate the power of youth to lead, innovate, and inspire.

"Powerful Kids" is more than just a collection of biographies. It is a celebration of the potential within every young person to make a difference. Through these stories, we hope to illuminate the ways in which passion, determination, and a commitment to social good can transcend age and experience. Each chapter is a reminder that the drive to improve our world often comes from the most unexpected places and that every one of us has the potential to contribute to positive change, regardless of our age.

As you read about these incredible young individuals, consider what drives you and how you can harness your own passions and talents to make a difference. Let these stories inspire you to take action, to dream bigger, and to believe in the power of youth to create a better, more just, and sustainable world. After all, the future is shaped by the actions we take today, and these powerful kids are leading the way.

Welcome to "Powerful Kids"—a journey into the lives of the young visionaries who are changing the world, one remarkable achievement at a time.

Chapter 1: Alex Deans

Alex Deans is a fascinating individual who has garnered attention for his exceptional achievements and contributions, particularly in the fields of technology and entrepreneurship. Born in 1999, Deans rose to prominence at a remarkably young age, showcasing remarkable ingenuity, vision, and determination. From developing innovative projects to founding successful companies, his journey is one of inspiration and admiration.

Early Life and Education

Born and raised in Ontario, Canada, Alex Deans exhibited an early aptitude for technology and innovation. His passion for creating and problem-solving became evident during his formative years, where he displayed a keen interest in computers, programming, and robotics. His parents, recognizing his talents, nurtured his curiosity and provided him with opportunities to explore his interests further.

Deans' educational journey played a crucial role in shaping his future endeavors. He attended reputable institutions where he could delve deeper into his passion for technology. While specific details about his educational background may vary, it's evident that Deans pursued a path that allowed him to develop the skills necessary to thrive in the competitive world of tech entrepreneurship.

Entrepreneurial Ventures

Deans' entrepreneurial journey began at a remarkably young age, reflecting his ambition and innovative spirit. One of his early notable projects was the development of a prosthetic hand using 3D printing technology. This endeavor showcased his commitment to leveraging technology for social good, as the prosthetic hand was designed to be affordable and accessible, particularly for individuals in underserved communities.

Building on this success, Deans continued to explore new avenues for innovation. He founded his first company, which focused on developing educational robotics kits for children. These kits aimed to inspire young minds and cultivate an interest in STEM (Science, Technology, Engineering, and Mathematics) fields from an early age. Deans' entrepreneurial acumen and passion for education were evident in this endeavor, as he sought to bridge the gap between technology and learning.

As Deans' reputation grew, so did his ventures. He embarked on various projects that showcased his versatility and vision. Whether it was creating immersive virtual reality experiences or developing cutting-edge software solutions, Deans demonstrated a knack for identifying emerging trends and harnessing technology to address real-world challenges.

Impact and Recognition

Deans' contributions have not gone unnoticed. His innovative projects and entrepreneurial success have earned him recognition and accolades from various quarters. He has been featured in numerous media outlets, where his story has inspired countless individuals, particularly young aspiring entrepreneurs.

Beyond media coverage, Deans' impact extends to the broader tech community. He has become a role model for young innovators, demonstrating that age is no barrier to making a significant difference in the world of technology and entrepreneurship. His willingness to share his knowledge and experiences has helped mentor and inspire the next generation of innovators.

Future Prospects

As Alex Deans continues on his entrepreneurial journey, the future holds immense promise. His passion for technology, coupled with his drive to make a positive impact, positions him as a formidable force in the tech industry. Whether it's developing groundbreaking innovations or spearheading initiatives to empower others, Deans' contributions are sure to leave a lasting legacy.

In conclusion, Alex Deans represents the epitome of a young visionary who has leveraged his passion for technology and entrepreneurship to effect meaningful change. From his early ventures to his current pursuits, Deans' journey serves as an inspiration to aspiring innovators worldwide. As he continues to push the boundaries of what's possible, one can only anticipate the incredible innovations and achievements that lie ahead for this remarkable individual.

Chapter 2: Gitanjali Rao

Gitanjali Rao is a name that has captivated the world with her intelligence, creativity, and passion for making a positive difference. Born in 2005, Rao is an Indian-American scientist, inventor, and advocate for STEM education, known for her groundbreaking innovations and commitment to addressing pressing global challenges. From her early childhood to her current endeavors, Rao's journey is a testament to the power of curiosity, perseverance, and innovation.

Early Life and Inspiration

Gitanjali Rao was born in Colorado, USA, to Indian immigrant parents. From a young age, she displayed a natural curiosity about the world around her, often asking questions and conducting experiments to satisfy her thirst for knowledge. Rao credits her parents and teachers for nurturing her inquisitive nature and encouraging her to pursue her interests in science and technology.

One of the pivotal moments in Rao's life came when she learned about the Flint water crisis, where the residents of Flint, Michigan, were exposed to lead-contaminated water. Deeply troubled by the situation, Rao felt compelled to take action. This experience ignited her passion for using science and technology to address real-world problems, setting her on a path of innovation and advocacy.

Innovation and Accomplishments

Rao's innovative spirit led her to develop groundbreaking solutions to some of society's most pressing challenges. At the age of 11, she gained widespread recognition for inventing a device called "Tethys," which uses carbon nanotubes to detect lead in water more efficiently and affordably than traditional methods. Tethys earned Rao the title of "America's Top Young Scientist" in the 2017 Discovery Education 3M Young Scientist Challenge, catapulting her into the spotlight and inspiring millions around the world.

Building on the success of Tethys, Rao continued to innovate in various fields, ranging from environmental science to public health. She developed other inventions, including a device to detect opioid addiction in its early stages and an app to combat cyberbullying by using artificial intelligence to analyze social media posts for signs of harassment.

Rao's achievements have not gone unnoticed. She has received numerous awards and honors for her work, including being named to Forbes' "30 Under 30" list and TIME magazine's "TIME100 Next" list, which recognizes rising stars who are shaping the future of their respective fields. Additionally, she has been invited to speak at prestigious events and conferences, where she shares her insights and inspires others to pursue their passions in STEM.

Advocacy and Outreach

Beyond her inventions, Gitanjali Rao is a passionate advocate for STEM education and youth empowerment. She believes in the importance of providing opportunities for young people, especially girls and underrepresented minorities, to pursue careers in science, technology, engineering, and mathematics.

Rao actively engages in outreach efforts to inspire the next generation of innovators. She speaks at schools, community events, and conferences, sharing her story and encouraging students to embrace their creativity and curiosity. Through her advocacy work, she aims to break down barriers and foster a more inclusive and diverse STEM community.

Future Endeavors

As Gitanjali Rao continues her journey, the future holds limitless possibilities. With her passion for innovation, dedication to making a positive impact, and unwavering commitment to solving global challenges, Rao is poised to achieve even greater feats in the years to come.

Whether it's developing new inventions, advocating for STEM education, or using her platform to amplify the voices of young changemakers, Rao's influence will undoubtedly continue to grow. Her story serves as an inspiration to aspiring scientists, inventors, and activists worldwide, reminding us all of the power of curiosity, perseverance, and innovation to change the world for the better.

Conclusion

In conclusion, Gitanjali Rao is a remarkable individual whose journey exemplifies the transformative power of curiosity, creativity, and determination. From her early experiences to her current endeavors, Rao has demonstrated a remarkable ability to innovate, inspire, and effect positive change. As she continues to push the boundaries of what's possible, one thing is certain: the world is better because of individuals like Gitanjali Rao who dare to dream big and make a difference.

Chapter 3: Nkosi Johnson

Nkosi Johnson remains an iconic figure in the global fight against HIV/AIDS, known not only for his courageous battle with the disease but also for his advocacy and activism that brought global attention to the plight of children living with HIV/AIDS in South Africa and beyond. Born Xolani Nkosi in 1989, he was thrust into the spotlight at a young age due to his diagnosis with HIV/AIDS, becoming a symbol of hope, resilience, and compassion in the face of adversity.

Early Life and Diagnosis

Nkosi Johnson was born to a South African mother, Nonthlanthla Daphne Nkosi, who was HIV-positive, and an unknown father. He was diagnosed with HIV/AIDS at birth, having contracted the virus from his mother. Despite being born into challenging circumstances, Nkosi's early years were marked by love and support from his adoptive mother, Gail Johnson, who provided him with the care and nurturing he needed to thrive.

Nkosi's diagnosis with HIV/AIDS came at a time when the disease was heavily stigmatized, particularly in South Africa, where misinformation and discrimination were rampant. However, rather than succumbing to despair, Nkosi and his family chose to confront the disease with courage and resilience, determined to live life to the fullest despite the challenges they faced.

Advocacy and Activism

As Nkosi grew older, he became increasingly aware of the stigma and discrimination faced by people living with HIV/AIDS, especially children like himself. He recognized the need to speak out and advocate for the rights of those affected by the disease, particularly children who often faced neglect, discrimination, and lack of access to essential healthcare and support services.

Nkosi's advocacy and activism gained international attention when, at the age of 11, he delivered a powerful speech at the 13th

International AIDS Conference held in Durban, South Africa, in 2000. In his speech, Nkosi eloquently described his experiences living with HIV/AIDS and called for greater awareness, compassion, and action to address the epidemic. His impassioned plea touched the hearts of millions worldwide and galvanized support for the global fight against HIV/AIDS.

Impact and Legacy

Nkosi Johnson's impact extended far beyond his speech at the AIDS conference. He became a symbol of hope and inspiration for people living with HIV/AIDS around the world, demonstrating that the disease did not define him and that individuals affected by it deserved love, respect, and dignity.

Tragically, Nkosi passed away on June 1, 2001, at the age of 12, due to complications related to AIDS. However, his legacy lived on, inspiring countless individuals to continue the fight against HIV/AIDS and to advocate for the rights and well-being of those affected by the disease.

In honor of his memory, the Nkosi Johnson Memorial Fund was established to continue his work and support initiatives aimed at improving the lives of children living with HIV/AIDS in South Africa. Additionally, the Nkosi's Haven organization, named after Nkosi himself, provides care, support, and advocacy for women and children affected by HIV/AIDS in South Africa.

Impact on HIV/AIDS Awareness and Policy

Nkosi Johnson's advocacy and activism had a profound impact on HIV/AIDS awareness and policy, both in South Africa and globally. His courage and determination helped to break down stigma and discrimination surrounding the disease, opening up conversations and fostering greater understanding and compassion for those affected by it.

In South Africa, Nkosi's legacy contributed to significant changes in HIV/AIDS policy and programming. His advocacy played a role in shaping the country's response to the epidemic, leading to improved access to antiretroviral treatment, increased support for HIV/AIDS prevention and education initiatives, and greater recognition of the rights of people living with HIV/AIDS.

Continuing the Fight

Despite his untimely passing, Nkosi Johnson's legacy continues to inspire individuals and organizations around the world to join the fight against HIV/AIDS. His message of compassion, resilience, and hope resonates with people of all ages and backgrounds, reminding us of the power of one individual to make a difference in the world.

In conclusion, Nkosi Johnson's life and legacy serve as a testament to the strength of the human spirit and the importance of compassion and advocacy in the face of adversity. Through his courage, determination, and unwavering commitment to making a difference, Nkosi Johnson touched the lives of millions and left an indelible mark on the global fight against HIV/AIDS. Though he may be gone, his legacy lives on, inspiring us all to continue the fight until AIDS is eradicated and every person affected by the disease receives the care, support, and dignity they deserve.

Chapter 4: Malala Yousafzai

Malala Yousafzai is a globally renowned activist, advocate for girls' education, and the youngest-ever Nobel Prize laureate. Her remarkable journey from a young girl in Pakistan's Swat Valley to an international symbol of courage and resilience has inspired millions around the world. In this detailed exploration, we'll delve into Malala's early life, her activism, the assassination attempt that nearly took her life, her continued advocacy, and the lasting impact she has had on education and human rights globally.

Early Life and Education

Malala Yousafzai was born on July 12, 1997, in Mingora, Swat Valley, Pakistan. Growing up, Malala was influenced by her father, Ziauddin Yousafzai, an educator and activist who ran a girls' school in their hometown. Ziauddin's commitment to education and his progressive views on gender equality deeply influenced Malala's own beliefs and aspirations.

Despite facing threats and intimidation from the Taliban, who sought to impose their extremist ideology and restrict girls' education in the region, Malala remained steadfast in her pursuit of knowledge. She attended her father's school and became increasingly vocal about the importance of education for all children, regardless of gender.

Activism for Girls' Education

Malala's activism gained international attention when, at the age of 11, she began anonymously writing a blog for BBC Urdu under the pseudonym Gul Makai. In her blog, Malala documented life under Taliban rule in Swat Valley and highlighted the challenges faced by girls who were denied access to education.

As Malala's profile grew, she became a prominent advocate for girls' education, speaking out against the Taliban's oppressive policies and calling for equal rights and opportunities for all children. Her courage and eloquence captured the world's attention and earned her numerous accolades and awards for her advocacy work.

Assassination Attempt and Recovery

Tragically, Malala's activism made her a target of the Taliban. On October 9, 2012, while returning home from school, Malala was shot in the head by a Taliban gunman in an assassination attempt intended to silence her and deter others from speaking out against the militant group's atrocities.

Miraculously, Malala survived the attack and was airlifted to the United Kingdom for emergency medical treatment. She underwent multiple surgeries and intensive rehabilitation, during which she remained resolute in her determination to continue her advocacy work for girls' education.

Global Impact and Recognition

Malala's resilience in the face of adversity and her unwavering commitment to education and human rights captured the world's imagination. She became a symbol of hope and courage, inspiring millions with her message of empowerment and equality.

In recognition of her advocacy, Malala was awarded the Nobel Peace Prize in 2014, becoming the youngest-ever recipient of the prestigious award at the age of 17. The Nobel Committee praised her "heroic struggle" for girls' right to education and her "courageous and dangerous fight" against the suppression of children.

Continued Advocacy and Leadership

Following her recovery, Malala continued to champion girls' education and human rights through the Malala Fund, an organization she co-founded with her father. The Malala Fund works to ensure that every girl has access to 12 years of free, safe, and quality education, advocating for policy changes, funding initiatives, and grassroots programs to support girls' education around the world.

Malala's advocacy has led to tangible results, including increased awareness of the importance of girls' education, changes in government policies, and improvements in access to schooling for girls in some of the world's most marginalized communities. Her tireless efforts have helped shine a spotlight on the barriers that prevent millions of girls from receiving an education and have inspired action to address these challenges.

Legacy and Inspiration

Malala Yousafzai's legacy extends far beyond her remarkable achievements and accolades. She has inspired a new generation of activists and change-makers to speak out against injustice, advocate for equality, and work towards a more just and equitable world.

Malala's story reminds us of the power of one individual to make a difference, even in the face of seemingly insurmountable odds. Her courage, resilience, and unwavering commitment to education and human rights serve as a beacon of hope for millions around the world, demonstrating that even the smallest voices can spark meaningful change.

In conclusion, Malala Yousafzai's journey from a young girl in Swat Valley to a global advocate for girls' education is a testament to the transformative power of education, activism, and resilience. Her story serves as a reminder of the importance of standing up for what is right, even in the face of adversity, and of the immense impact that one person can have on the world. Malala's legacy will continue to inspire future generations to strive for a better, more inclusive world where every child has the opportunity to fulfill their potential through education.

Chapter 5: Mikaila Ulmer

Mikaila Ulmer is a remarkable young entrepreneur, conservationist, and advocate for sustainability, best known as the founder and CEO of Me & the Bees Lemonade. Her inspiring journey from a lemonade stand to a successful businesswoman and environmental activist has captured the hearts and minds of people around the world. In this comprehensive exploration, we'll delve into Mikaila's background, the story behind her lemonade company, her commitment to saving bees, and her broader impact on entrepreneurship and environmentalism.

Early Life and Inspiration

Mikaila Ulmer was born on April 18, 2005, in Austin, Texas, USA. Her passion for entrepreneurship and environmentalism emerged at a young age, inspired by her family's commitment to both business and conservation. Mikaila's great-grandmother, Helen, was a beekeeper, and Mikaila herself developed an early fascination with bees and their crucial role in ecosystems.

The Lemonade Stand and Bee Mission

At the age of four, Mikaila was stung by a bee, an experience that sparked her curiosity about these pollinators and their importance to the environment. Determined to learn more, Mikaila began researching bees and discovered the alarming decline in bee populations due to habitat loss, pesticide use, and climate change.

Inspired to take action, Mikaila decided to combine her love of bees with her passion for entrepreneurship by starting a lemonade stand. She experimented with different recipes, eventually creating a unique blend of lemonade sweetened with honey, which she named "Me & the Bees Lemonade." Mikaila's lemonade not only tasted delicious but also served as a platform to raise awareness about the plight of bees and the importance of conservation.

Growth and Success

Mikaila's lemonade stand quickly gained popularity in her local community, thanks to the unique concept and the quality of her product. As word spread about Me & the Bees Lemonade, Mikaila's business began to grow, attracting attention from customers, retailers, and the media.

One of the key milestones in Mikaila's entrepreneurial journey came when she appeared on the television show "Shark Tank" in 2015. Her confident pitch and compelling story impressed the judges, leading to a partnership with FUBU CEO Daymond John, who invested $60,000 in Me & the Bees Lemonade in exchange for a 25% stake in the company.

With Daymond John's support and guidance, Me & the Bees Lemonade expanded its distribution, securing partnerships with major retailers such as Whole Foods Market and Wegmans. Mikaila's lemonade became available in stores across the United States, further raising awareness about the importance of bees and sustainable agriculture.

Commitment to Sustainability and Social Impact

Beyond building a successful business, Mikaila remains committed to making a positive impact on the environment and society. Me & the Bees Lemonade is dedicated to using natural, sustainably sourced ingredients, including honey from local beekeepers who practice ethical and environmentally friendly beekeeping methods.

In addition to promoting bee conservation, Mikaila's company supports social causes and community initiatives. A portion of the proceeds from Me & the Bees Lemonade sales goes towards organizations working to protect bees and their habitats, as well as programs that empower young entrepreneurs and promote education in underserved communities.

Recognition and Awards

Mikaila Ulmer's entrepreneurial achievements and commitment to social and environmental responsibility have earned her widespread recognition and numerous awards. She has been featured in major media outlets, including Forbes, TIME, and CNN, and has received accolades for her leadership and innovation.

In 2017, Mikaila was named to TIME magazine's list of the "30 Most Influential Teens" for her entrepreneurial success and activism. She has also been honored with awards such as the NAACP Image Award for Outstanding Literary Work by a Youth/Teen and the Young Futurist Award from The Root.

Future Endeavors and Impact

As Mikaila Ulmer continues her entrepreneurial journey, the future holds immense promise for both her and Me & the Bees Lemonade. With her passion for sustainability, innovation, and social impact, Mikaila is poised to inspire future generations of entrepreneurs and environmentalists to create businesses that make a difference in the world.

Through Me & the Bees Lemonade, Mikaila has not only raised awareness about the importance of bees and sustainable agriculture but also demonstrated the power of business as a force for positive change. Her story serves as a reminder that even the smallest actions, such as starting a lemonade stand, can have a ripple effect and contribute to building a more sustainable and equitable world.

Conclusion

In conclusion, Mikaila Ulmer's journey from a lemonade stand to a successful businesswoman and environmental activist is a testament to the power of passion, innovation, and social responsibility. Through Me & the Bees Lemonade, Mikaila has not only built a thriving business but also raised awareness about critical issues such as bee conservation and sustainability.

Mikaila's story serves as an inspiration to aspiring entrepreneurs and changemakers, demonstrating that age is no barrier to making a meaningful impact on the world. With her vision, determination, and commitment to creating positive change, Mikaila Ulmer is truly a beacon of hope for future generations.

18

Chapter 6: Caine Monroy

Caine Monroy became a household name overnight thanks to his incredible creativity, entrepreneurial spirit, and a cardboard arcade that captured the hearts of people worldwide. His story is a testament to the power of imagination, perseverance, and the impact that one individual can have on their community and beyond.

Early Life and Inspiration

Caine Monroy was born on March 1, 2000, in Los Angeles, California, to George and Nirvan Mullick. Growing up, Caine displayed a keen interest in building and creating, often spending hours constructing elaborate structures and inventions out of cardboard boxes and other recycled materials.

Caine's passion for tinkering and inventing was nurtured by his father, George, who encouraged his son's creativity and provided him with the tools and resources to bring his ideas to life. Together, they would spend weekends working on various projects in their family's auto parts store in East Los Angeles.

The Cardboard Arcade

In the summer of 2011, when Caine was just nine years old, he embarked on his most ambitious project yet—a cardboard arcade built entirely from recycled materials. Using cardboard boxes, tape, and other found objects, Caine transformed a corner of his father's auto parts store into a fully functional arcade, complete with games, prizes, and tickets.

Caine's cardboard arcade featured a variety of games and attractions, including a basketball hoop, a claw machine, and a miniature soccer table. Each game was meticulously designed and constructed by Caine himself, showcasing his ingenuity and attention to detail.

Caine's Big Break

Despite his creativity and enthusiasm, Caine's cardboard arcade initially attracted little attention from customers. However, that all changed when filmmaker Nirvan Mullick stumbled upon the arcade while visiting the auto parts store to purchase a door handle for his car.

Impressed by Caine's ingenuity and entrepreneurial spirit, Mullick struck up a conversation with the young boy and asked if he could make a short film about his arcade. Caine eagerly agreed, and over the course of a few weeks, Mullick documented the story of Caine's Arcade, capturing the magic and charm of the cardboard arcade and the remarkable young boy behind it.

The Power of Social Media

In April 2012, Mullick released a short film titled "Caine's Arcade," which quickly went viral after being shared on social media platforms like YouTube and Facebook. The heartwarming story of Caine and his cardboard arcade resonated with millions of people around the world, sparking an outpouring of support and admiration for the young entrepreneur.

Viewers were inspired by Caine's creativity, perseverance, and unwavering optimism in the face of adversity. They were also touched by the bond between Caine and his father, George, who had supported and encouraged his son's dreams from the very beginning.

Caine's Arcade Day

In response to the overwhelming support generated by the film, Mullick organized a global event called "Caine's Arcade Day" to celebrate Caine's creativity and raise funds for his college education. On October 6, 2012, communities around the world hosted cardboard arcade events, inviting participants to build and play games inspired by Caine's arcade.

The inaugural Caine's Arcade Day was a resounding success, with thousands of people coming together to celebrate creativity, entrepreneurship, and community. The event raised over $240,000 for the Caine's Arcade Scholarship Fund, which was established to support the educational aspirations of Caine and other children like him.

Impact and Legacy

Caine's story captured the hearts of people worldwide and inspired a wave of creativity and entrepreneurship in communities everywhere. His cardboard arcade became a symbol of hope and possibility, demonstrating that with a little imagination and ingenuity, anything is possible.

In addition to raising funds for his college education, Caine's Arcade also inspired the creation of the Imagination Foundation, a nonprofit organization dedicated to fostering creativity and entrepreneurship in children around the world. The Imagination Foundation provides resources, support, and inspiration to young innovators, helping them turn their ideas into reality.

Caine's Continued Journey

Since the success of Caine's Arcade, Caine Monroy has continued to pursue his passion for creativity and innovation. He has appeared on talk shows, given keynote speeches at conferences, and shared his story with audiences around the world.

In 2014, Caine was invited to speak at the TEDxTeen conference in New York City, where he shared his experiences and insights as a young entrepreneur. He spoke about the importance of following your passions, embracing failure as a learning opportunity, and believing in yourself even when others doubt you.

Conclusion

In conclusion, Caine Monroy's story is a testament to the power of creativity, perseverance, and the human spirit. From humble beginnings in a cardboard arcade to global recognition and acclaim, Caine's journey has inspired millions of people around the world to pursue their dreams and embrace their inner innovator.

Through his creativity and entrepreneurial spirit, Caine has shown that age is no barrier to making a positive impact on the world. His story serves as a reminder that with passion, determination, and a little bit of cardboard, anything is possible. Caine Monroy's legacy will continue to inspire future generations of innovators and changemakers for years to come.

Chapter 7: Peyton Robertson

Peyton Robertson is a young inventor and entrepreneur whose innovative creations have garnered international acclaim and recognition. From his early childhood experiments to his groundbreaking inventions, Peyton's journey is a testament to the power of curiosity, creativity, and determination. In this comprehensive exploration, we'll delve into Peyton's background, his notable inventions, his entrepreneurial ventures, and the impact he has had on the world of innovation and technology.

Early Life and Inspiration

Peyton Robertson was born on January 1, 2001, in Fort Lauderdale, Florida, USA. From a young age, Peyton displayed a natural curiosity and aptitude for science and engineering. Inspired by his father, who was an engineer, Peyton began conducting experiments and building contraptions in his backyard workshop.

As he grew older, Peyton's passion for invention and innovation only intensified. He was fascinated by the process of problem-solving and the opportunity to use science and technology to address real-world challenges. Peyton's parents encouraged his interests and provided him with the support and resources he needed to pursue his dreams.

Notable Inventions

Throughout his childhood and adolescence, Peyton Robertson developed a series of innovative inventions that showcased his ingenuity and creativity. One of his earliest inventions, created when he was just 11 years old, was a sandbag alternative designed to protect homes and properties from flooding. Peyton's sandbag alternative utilized a polymer-based material that expanded when wet, providing a lightweight and effective solution for flood prevention.

Another notable invention by Peyton Robertson is the "QuickWick," a highly absorbent material capable of quickly soaking up oil spills on water surfaces. Inspired by the devastating Deepwater Horizon oil spill in 2010, Peyton recognized the need for a more efficient and environmentally friendly cleanup solution. The QuickWick material, which he developed at the age of 14, demonstrated remarkable absorbency and effectiveness in laboratory tests, earning Peyton widespread recognition and praise for his ingenuity.

Awards and Recognition

Peyton Robertson's innovative inventions have earned him numerous awards and accolades from prestigious organizations and competitions. He has been recognized for his creativity, ingenuity, and commitment to making a positive impact on the world.

One of Peyton's most significant achievements came in 2013 when he won the grand prize at the Discovery Education 3M Young Scientist Challenge. His project, which focused on developing a more effective sandbag alternative, impressed the judges with its innovation, practicality, and potential for real-world application. Peyton's success at the Young Scientist Challenge catapulted him into the national spotlight and solidified his reputation as a rising star in the world of science and engineering.

Entrepreneurial Ventures

In addition to his inventive prowess, Peyton Robertson is also an aspiring entrepreneur with a keen interest in bringing his creations to market. He has founded several startups aimed at commercializing his inventions and developing new technologies to address pressing global challenges.

One of Peyton's entrepreneurial ventures is "Rethink," a company he founded to develop innovative solutions for environmental sustainability and disaster preparedness. Through Rethink, Peyton aims to leverage technology and engineering to create products and services that mitigate the impact of natural disasters, protect the environment, and improve the resilience of communities worldwide.

Impact and Legacy

Peyton Robertson's impact extends beyond his individual inventions and entrepreneurial endeavors. He serves as a role model and inspiration to aspiring inventors and innovators, demonstrating the potential of young people to make meaningful contributions to society through science and technology.

By tackling complex problems and developing practical solutions, Peyton has shown that age is no barrier to innovation and entrepreneurship. His story serves as a reminder that with passion, perseverance, and a willingness to think outside the box, anything is possible.

Future Endeavors

As Peyton Robertson continues his journey as an inventor and entrepreneur, the future holds limitless possibilities. With his boundless creativity, determination, and commitment to making a positive impact, Peyton is poised to achieve even greater feats in the years to come.

Whether it's developing new inventions, founding startups, or advocating for environmental sustainability, Peyton's contributions are sure to leave a lasting legacy. His innovative spirit and dedication to solving global challenges serve as a beacon of hope for the next generation of inventors and changemakers, inspiring them to dream big and pursue their passions with courage and conviction.

Conclusion

In conclusion, Peyton Robertson is a remarkable young inventor and entrepreneur whose ingenuity and creativity have captivated the world. From his early childhood experiments to his groundbreaking inventions, Peyton's journey exemplifies the power of curiosity, innovation, and perseverance.

Through his inventive creations and entrepreneurial ventures, Peyton has demonstrated the transformative potential of science and technology to address some of the most pressing challenges facing humanity. His story serves as an inspiration to young people everywhere, reminding them that they have the power to change the world with their ideas and inventions. As Peyton continues to pursue his passion for innovation and entrepreneurship, one thing is certain: the future is brighter because of visionaries like him.

Chapter 8: Kiran Sridhar

Kiran Sridhar is a name synonymous with innovation, social impact, and youth empowerment. As the founder and CEO of Waste Ventures India, he has made significant strides in transforming waste management in India and beyond. Sridhar's journey from a young entrepreneur to a leading figure in the sustainability space is a testament to his passion, vision, and commitment to creating positive change. In this detailed exploration, we'll delve into Sridhar's background, his innovative initiatives, his impact on waste management, and his broader influence on entrepreneurship and sustainability.

Early Life and Education

Kiran Sridhar was born and raised in Hyderabad, India, where he developed a keen interest in environmental issues from a young age. His upbringing instilled in him a sense of responsibility towards the planet and a desire to address the pressing challenges of waste management and environmental degradation.

Sridhar's educational background includes a degree in Environmental Science and Policy from Duke University in the United States. It was during his time at Duke that he began to explore innovative solutions to environmental problems and envision ways to make a meaningful impact in his home country of India.

Founding Waste Ventures India

In 2011, at the age of 21, Kiran Sridhar founded Waste Ventures India with a mission to revolutionize waste management in India's urban areas. Recognizing the urgent need for sustainable solutions to the country's growing waste problem, Sridhar set out to create a social enterprise that would not only address environmental challenges but also generate economic opportunities for marginalized communities.

Waste Ventures India operates on a model that integrates waste collection, segregation, and recycling, while also providing employment and livelihood opportunities to waste pickers and other informal workers. By formalizing the waste management sector and creating value from waste materials, Sridhar's initiative has the potential to transform the lives of millions while also mitigating the environmental impact of waste.

Innovative Solutions and Technologies

Under Kiran Sridhar's leadership, Waste Ventures India has pioneered several innovative solutions and technologies to improve waste management practices and increase efficiency. One such initiative is the deployment of IoT (Internet of Things) sensors and data analytics to optimize waste collection routes and schedules, reducing fuel consumption and carbon emissions while improving service delivery.

Additionally, Waste Ventures India has introduced innovative recycling technologies, such as pyrolysis and composting, to convert organic waste into valuable resources like biochar and organic fertilizer. These technologies not only divert waste from landfills but also create opportunities for circular economy solutions that promote resource conservation and sustainable development.

Impact on Waste Management

Since its founding, Waste Ventures India has made significant strides in transforming waste management practices in urban areas across India. By formalizing the sector, providing training and support to waste pickers, and implementing innovative technologies, Sridhar's initiative has improved waste collection rates, reduced environmental pollution, and created new economic opportunities for marginalized communities.

The impact of Waste Ventures India extends beyond waste management to encompass broader social and environmental benefits. By promoting sustainable consumption and production patterns, reducing greenhouse gas emissions, and fostering community engagement, Sridhar's initiative is contributing to India's sustainable development goals and inspiring similar efforts around the world.

Recognition and Awards

Kiran Sridhar's innovative work in waste management has earned him widespread recognition and numerous awards from prestigious organizations and institutions. He has been honored for his leadership, entrepreneurship, and commitment to social and environmental sustainability.

One of Sridhar's most notable achievements is being named a Forbes 30 Under 30 Asia honoree in the Social Entrepreneurship category. This prestigious accolade highlights his contributions to creating positive social impact and driving change in the field of waste management.

Influence on Entrepreneurship and Sustainability

As a young entrepreneur and sustainability advocate, Kiran Sridhar serves as a role model and inspiration to aspiring changemakers around the world. His innovative approach to addressing environmental challenges and his commitment to creating shared value through social enterprise have inspired a new generation of entrepreneurs to pursue ventures that prioritize people, planet, and profit.

Sridhar's success with Waste Ventures India has also demonstrated the potential for business to be a force for positive change, driving innovation, creating jobs, and advancing sustainability goals. By showcasing the economic viability of sustainable business models and demonstrating the importance of stakeholder engagement and collaboration, Sridhar has helped to shape the future of entrepreneurship in India and beyond.

Future Endeavors

As Kiran Sridhar continues his journey as a social entrepreneur and sustainability leader, the future holds immense promise. With his passion for innovation, dedication to social impact, and commitment to creating a more sustainable world, Sridhar is poised to make even greater strides in the years to come.

Whether it's expanding Waste Ventures India's reach to new cities and regions, scaling up innovative waste management technologies, or advocating for policy changes that support sustainability and social inclusion, Sridhar's impact will continue to be felt far and wide.

Conclusion

In conclusion, Kiran Sridhar is a visionary leader whose entrepreneurial spirit and commitment to sustainability have made a lasting impact on waste management and environmental conservation in India and beyond. Through Waste Ventures India, he has demonstrated the transformative potential of social enterprise to address pressing environmental challenges while also creating economic opportunities and empowering marginalized communities.

Sridhar's innovative approach, dedication to social impact, and leadership in the field of waste management serve as a shining example of how business can be a force for positive change. As he continues to pioneer new solutions, inspire others, and drive progress towards a more sustainable future, Kiran Sridhar's legacy will endure as a beacon of hope and inspiration for generations to come.

Chapter 9: Sebastian de la Cruz

Sebastián de la Cruz is a multifaceted young talent whose journey embodies the spirit of resilience, diversity, and cultural pride. From his early beginnings as a talented singer to his rise to fame on a national stage, Sebastián's story is one of overcoming adversity and embracing his heritage. In this comprehensive exploration, we'll delve into Sebastián's background, his breakthrough moment, his impact on cultural representation, and his continued evolution as an artist and advocate.

Early Life and Introduction to Music

Sebastián de la Cruz was born on July 9, 2004, in San Antonio, Texas, to Mexican-American parents. From a young age, Sebastián showed a natural talent for music, often singing and performing for family and friends. His parents, recognizing his passion and potential, encouraged him to pursue his musical interests and provided him with opportunities to develop his skills.

At the age of 4, Sebastián began singing in church and participating in local talent shows and competitions. His powerful voice and charismatic stage presence quickly caught the attention of audiences, earning him recognition as a rising star in the San Antonio music scene.

Breakthrough Moment: America's Got Talent

Sebastián de la Cruz's breakthrough moment came in 2012 when he auditioned for the seventh season of the hit reality television show "America's Got Talent." At just 10 years old, Sebastián captivated the judges and audience with his rendition of the classic mariachi song "El Triste."

Despite facing initial skepticism and prejudice due to his young age and ethnic background, Sebastián's talent and authenticity shone through, earning him a standing ovation from the judges and praise for his vocal prowess and stage presence. His performance went viral, garnering millions of views on social media and catapulting Sebastián to national prominence.

Response to Criticism and Embracing Identity

Following his audition on "America's Got Talent," Sebastián de la Cruz faced backlash and criticism from some viewers who questioned his authenticity and suitability as a contestant. Some individuals expressed disbelief that a young Mexican-American boy could sing mariachi music with such skill and passion, while others made derogatory remarks about his ethnicity and appearance.

In response to the criticism, Sebastián remained poised and dignified, refusing to let negative comments detract from his love of music and pride in his heritage. He embraced his identity as a Mexican-American and continued to perform mariachi music with confidence and authenticity, becoming a symbol of cultural pride and resilience for millions of people around the world.

Cultural Representation and Impact

Sebastián de la Cruz's appearance on "America's Got Talent" had a profound impact on cultural representation and diversity in the media. As one of the few Mexican-American contestants on the show at the time, Sebastián's presence challenged stereotypes and misconceptions about Latinx identity and showcased the rich cultural heritage of Mexican-American communities.

Through his performances of mariachi music, Sebastián brought attention to a traditional art form that is deeply rooted in Mexican culture and history. He introduced audiences to the beauty and complexity of mariachi music, inspiring a newfound appreciation for this cherished musical tradition.

Continued Evolution as an Artist

Since his appearance on "America's Got Talent," Sebastián de la Cruz has continued to pursue his passion for music and performance while also expanding his artistic horizons. He has released original music, collaborated with other artists, and performed at events and venues across the country.

In addition to his music career, Sebastián has also explored other creative pursuits, including acting and modeling. He has appeared in commercials, television shows, and films, showcasing his versatility and charisma on screen.

Advocacy and Community Engagement

Beyond his artistic endeavors, Sebastián de la Cruz is also actively involved in advocacy and community engagement efforts. He uses his platform to raise awareness about issues affecting marginalized communities, including immigration, education, and cultural representation.

Sebastián is a vocal supporter of diversity and inclusion in the arts and entertainment industry, advocating for greater representation of Latinx voices and stories in mainstream media. He also participates in charitable initiatives and community events, using his influence to uplift and empower others.

Legacy and Inspiration

Sebastián de la Cruz's legacy extends far beyond his accomplishments as a singer and performer. He serves as a role model and inspiration to young people everywhere, demonstrating the importance of embracing one's heritage, pursuing one's passions, and standing up against prejudice and discrimination.

Through his music, advocacy, and community engagement, Sebastián has touched the lives of countless individuals and inspired positive change in the world. His resilience, authenticity, and commitment to cultural pride serve as a beacon of hope and empowerment for generations to come.

Conclusion

In conclusion, Sebastián de la Cruz's journey from a young singer to a cultural icon is a testament to the power of music, identity, and resilience. Through his talent, authenticity, and unwavering pride in his heritage, Sebastián has broken barriers, challenged stereotypes, and inspired millions around the world.

As he continues to evolve as an artist and advocate, Sebastián de la Cruz remains dedicated to using his voice to uplift and empower others. Whether performing on stage, speaking out against injustice, or engaging with his community, Sebastián's impact is felt far and wide, leaving an indelible mark on the world of music and beyond.

Chapter 10: Anne Frank

Anne Frank is one of the most widely known and celebrated Jewish victims of the Holocaust. Her diary, written while she and her family were in hiding during the Nazi occupation of the Netherlands, has become a symbol of hope, resilience, and the human spirit in the face of adversity. In this comprehensive exploration, we'll delve into Anne Frank's life, her diary, the circumstances of her hiding, her legacy, and the impact of her writings on the world.

Early Life and Background

Anne Frank was born Annelies Marie Frank on June 12, 1929, in Frankfurt, Germany, to Otto and Edith Frank. The Frank family was of Jewish descent, and Anne had an older sister named Margot. In 1933, with the rise of the Nazi party and the increasing persecution of Jews in Germany, the Frank family fled to Amsterdam, Netherlands, where Otto established a business.

Anne grew up in Amsterdam and attended a Montessori school. She was an intelligent and precocious child, known for her lively personality, love of writing, and strong sense of curiosity. Anne had dreams of becoming a writer or journalist, and she showed early talent in expressing her thoughts and feelings through words.

The Diary of Anne Frank

On her 13th birthday in 1942, Anne Frank received a red-and-white checkered diary as a gift from her parents. Little did she know that this diary would become one of the most important and enduring literary works of the 20th century. Anne began writing in her diary immediately, addressing it as "Kitty" and pouring out her thoughts, feelings, and observations about her life, her family, and the world around her.

In her diary, Anne Frank documented the challenges of living in hiding during the Nazi occupation of the Netherlands, as well as her hopes, dreams, and aspirations for the future. She wrote about the cramped quarters of the "Secret Annex," where her family and four others hid from Nazi persecution, and the constant fear of discovery by the authorities.

Life in Hiding

In July 1942, following an increase in anti-Jewish measures in Amsterdam, the Frank family went into hiding in the annex of Otto Frank's business premises at Prinsengracht 263. They were joined by another Jewish family, the van Pels, and later by a dentist named Fritz Pfeffer. For over two years, the eight inhabitants of the Secret Annex lived in constant fear of discovery, relying on the courage and resourcefulness of Otto Frank's employees to bring them food and supplies.

Despite the difficult conditions of hiding, Anne Frank remained optimistic and determined to maintain a sense of normalcy. She continued to write in her diary, chronicling the daily struggles and triumphs of life in confinement. She also developed close bonds with the other inhabitants of the annex, finding solace and companionship amidst the uncertainty and fear.

Discovery and Arrest

Tragically, the hiding place of the Frank family and their companions was betrayed to the Nazis in August 1944. The occupants of the annex were arrested by the Gestapo and taken to various concentration camps. Anne, her sister Margot, and their mother Edith were sent to Auschwitz-Birkenau, where they were separated from Otto Frank, who was sent to a different camp.

In January 1945, Anne and Margot were transferred to the Bergen-Belsen concentration camp, where they both succumbed to typhus and died within weeks of each other, in February or March 1945. Their mother, Edith, also perished in Auschwitz. Otto Frank, the sole survivor of the family, returned to Amsterdam after the war and was given Anne's diary by Miep Gies, one of the Dutch citizens who had helped hide the Frank family.

Publication and Legacy

After reading his daughter's diary, Otto Frank was deeply moved by its contents and resolved to fulfill Anne's wish to become a writer. He worked tirelessly to edit and prepare the diary for publication, eventually securing a publishing deal with Contact Publishers in Amsterdam.

The diary of Anne Frank, titled "Het Achterhuis" (The Secret Annex) in Dutch and later translated into English as "The Diary of a Young Girl," was first published in 1947. It quickly became an international bestseller, captivating readers with its honesty, insight, and humanity. Anne's diary has since been translated into over 70 languages and has sold millions of copies worldwide.

Impact and Influence

The diary of Anne Frank has had a profound impact on people of all ages and backgrounds, resonating with readers around the world for its universal themes of hope, resilience, and the enduring power of the human spirit. Anne's words have inspired generations to stand up against prejudice, intolerance, and injustice, and to work towards a more compassionate and inclusive society.

The Anne Frank House, located at Prinsengracht 263 in Amsterdam, has become a pilgrimage site for millions of visitors each year, offering a glimpse into the lives of Anne Frank and the other occupants of the Secret Annex. The museum preserves the memory of Anne Frank and serves as a testament to the horrors of the Holocaust, reminding visitors of the consequences of hatred and discrimination.

Anne Frank's Message

In her diary, Anne Frank wrote, "I still believe, in spite of everything, that people are truly good at heart." This message of hope and optimism, penned by a young girl in the darkest of times, continues to resonate with people around the world today. Anne's words remind us of the importance of empathy, compassion, and understanding in the face of adversity, and inspire us to strive for a better, more just world.

Conclusion

In conclusion, Anne Frank's diary stands as a testament to the enduring power of the human spirit and the importance of bearing witness to history. Through her words, Anne Frank has given a voice to the millions of victims of the Holocaust, ensuring that their stories are not forgotten and that their legacy lives on.

Anne's diary continues to inspire and educate people around the world, serving as a reminder of the consequences of intolerance, prejudice, and hatred. Her message of hope, resilience, and humanity resonates as strongly today as it did over 75 years ago, reminding us of the enduring power of the human spirit to overcome even the darkest of times.

Chapter 11: Iqbal Masih

Iqbal Masih was a symbol of courage, resilience, and advocacy in the fight against child labor. Born in Muridke, Pakistan, on April 12, 1983, Iqbal's life was tragically cut short, but his legacy continues to inspire and drive change around the world. In this detailed exploration, we'll delve into Iqbal Masih's early life, his experience as a child laborer, his remarkable escape from bondage, his advocacy for children's rights, and the enduring impact of his legacy on the global fight against child labor.

Early Life and Bonded Labor

Iqbal Masih was born into poverty in a small village in Punjab, Pakistan. At the tender age of four, he was sold into bonded labor by his parents to pay off a debt of around 600 rupees (approximately $12 USD). Bonded labor, also known as debt bondage, is a form of modern slavery in which people are forced to work to repay a debt, often under harsh and exploitative conditions.

For six years, Iqbal worked as a carpet weaver in a local carpet factory, enduring long hours, meager wages, and physical abuse. Despite the hardships he faced, Iqbal remained determined to break free from bondage and pursue a better life for himself and his family.

Escape and Advocacy

In 1992, at the age of 10, Iqbal Masih managed to escape from the carpet factory with the help of the Bonded Labor Liberation Front (BLLF), a Pakistani organization dedicated to combating child labor and bonded labor. After his escape, Iqbal joined the BLLF as an advocate for children's rights, determined to prevent other children from suffering the same fate he had endured.

Despite his young age, Iqbal became a powerful voice for change, speaking out against child labor and advocating for the rights of children around the world. He traveled to countries such as Sweden, the United States, and Canada, where he shared his story and raised awareness about the plight of child laborers in Pakistan and other countries.

International Recognition and Awards

Iqbal Masih's courageous advocacy efforts earned him international recognition and acclaim. He was awarded the Reebok Human Rights Award in 1994, which recognized his extraordinary courage and determination in the fight against child labor. He was also honored with the World's Children's Prize for the Rights of the Child in 2000, posthumously recognizing his contributions to the advancement of children's rights.

Impact and Legacy

Iqbal Masih's legacy continues to inspire and motivate individuals and organizations around the world to take action against child labor and exploitation. His story has raised awareness about the prevalence of child labor in many countries and has spurred efforts to address the root causes of the problem, including poverty, lack of education, and inadequate enforcement of labor laws.

In Pakistan, Iqbal's story has led to increased awareness and advocacy around the issue of bonded labor, prompting government officials and civil society organizations to take steps to combat this form of modern slavery. Efforts have been made to rescue and rehabilitate bonded laborers, provide access to education and vocational training, and strengthen legal protections for children's rights.

Continuing the Fight Against Child Labor

While significant progress has been made in the fight against child labor in recent years, millions of children around the world continue to be trapped in exploitative and hazardous work. The COVID-19 pandemic has further exacerbated the problem, pushing millions of families into poverty and forcing children out of school and into the workforce to help support their families.

To address the root causes of child labor and ensure the rights and well-being of all children, concerted efforts are needed at the local, national, and international levels. Governments, businesses, civil society organizations, and individuals must work together to eliminate child labor, promote access to education and social services, and create opportunities for sustainable livelihoods for vulnerable communities.

Conclusion

In conclusion, Iqbal Masih's life and legacy serve as a powerful reminder of the urgent need to end child labor and protect the rights and dignity of all children. Despite enduring unimaginable hardships, Iqbal remained steadfast in his commitment to justice and equality, using his voice to shine a light on the plight of child laborers around the world.

Through his advocacy and activism, Iqbal inspired millions of people to take action against child labor and exploitation, leaving an indelible mark on the global movement for children's rights. While Iqbal's life was tragically cut short, his legacy lives on, fueling the ongoing fight for a world where every child has the opportunity to grow up safe, healthy, and free from exploitation.

Chapter 12: Adora Svitak

Adora Svitak is a remarkable young author, speaker, and advocate for children's rights and education. Born on October 15, 1997, in Springfield, Oregon, Adora gained international recognition at a young age for her eloquent writing, insightful speeches, and passionate advocacy for youth empowerment. In this comprehensive exploration, we'll delve into Adora Svitak's background, her early achievements, her impact on education and activism, and her continued evolution as a voice for change.

Early Life and Passion for Writing

Adora Svitak's love for writing began at an early age. From the moment she could hold a pencil, she was scribbling stories and poems, eager to share her thoughts and ideas with the world. Encouraged by her parents and teachers, Adora honed her writing skills and developed a unique voice that captivated readers of all ages.

Prodigy and Author

At the age of seven, Adora Svitak published her first book, "Flying Fingers," a collection of short stories and poems that showcased her creativity and imagination. The book received critical acclaim and established Adora as a prodigious talent in the world of literature.

TED Talk and International Recognition

In 2010, at the age of 12, Adora Svitak delivered a TED Talk titled "What Adults Can Learn from Kids," which catapulted her to international fame. In her inspiring and thought-provoking speech, Adora challenged the audience to rethink their perceptions of children and to recognize the wisdom, creativity, and potential that young people possess.

Adora's TED Talk went viral, garnering millions of views and sparking a global conversation about the importance of listening to and empowering youth. Overnight, Adora became a symbol of hope and inspiration for children and adults alike, proving that age is no barrier to making a meaningful impact on the world.

Advocacy for Education and Youth Empowerment

Following her TED Talk, Adora Svitak emerged as a passionate advocate for education and youth empowerment. She traveled the world, speaking at conferences, schools, and events, where she shared her insights and experiences as a young writer and activist.

Adora's advocacy work focused on the importance of providing children and young people with opportunities to learn, grow, and express themselves. She emphasized the need for educational systems that nurture creativity, critical thinking, and innovation, and that empower students to become active agents of change in their communities and beyond.

Writing and Literary Career

In addition to her advocacy work, Adora Svitak continued to pursue her passion for writing. She published several more books, including "Reflections of a Teenage Author" and "Dancing Fingers," which further showcased her talent and versatility as a writer.

Adora's writing explores a wide range of themes and topics, from fantasy and adventure to social justice and human rights. She uses her platform to raise awareness about issues affecting young people and to inspire others to use their voices for positive change.

Impact on Education and Activism

Adora Svitak's impact on education and activism has been profound and far-reaching. Through her writing, speaking engagements, and advocacy work, she has inspired countless children, parents, educators, and policymakers to reexamine their beliefs and assumptions about youth and to prioritize the needs and aspirations of young people in their communities.

Adora's message of empowerment, resilience, and hope has resonated with audiences around the world, sparking a movement to transform education systems and create a more inclusive and equitable society for all. Her work has led to concrete changes in educational policies and practices, as well as increased recognition of the importance of youth participation and leadership in shaping the future.

Continued Evolution and Impact

As Adora Svitak has grown older, her activism and advocacy have evolved, but her commitment to creating positive change remains unwavering. She continues to speak out on issues such as climate change, gender equality, and social justice, using her platform to amplify the voices of marginalized communities and to advocate for a more just and sustainable world.

Adora's impact extends beyond her writing and speaking engagements to encompass her work as a mentor, role model, and leader in the global youth movement. She has inspired a new generation of young activists and changemakers to stand up for their beliefs, speak truth to power, and work together to build a brighter future for all.

Conclusion

In conclusion, Adora Svitak is a shining example of the power of youth to effect positive change in the world. From her early achievements as a prodigious writer to her impactful advocacy for education and youth empowerment, Adora has demonstrated the extraordinary potential of young people to make a difference and shape the course of history.

Through her writing, speaking engagements, and activism, Adora has inspired millions of people to believe in themselves, pursue their passions, and work together to create a more just, equitable, and sustainable world. Her legacy will endure as a beacon of hope and inspiration for generations to come, reminding us all of the transformative power of youth and the importance of listening to and uplifting the voices of young people everywhere.

Chapter 13: Tenzin Gyatso

Tenzin Gyatso, known as the 14th Dalai Lama, is one of the world's most influential spiritual leaders and advocates for peace, compassion, and human rights. Born on July 6, 1935, in the small village of Taktser in northeastern Tibet, Tenzin Gyatso was recognized at the age of two as the reincarnation of his predecessor, the 13th Dalai Lama. From a young age, he was destined to play a pivotal role in the spiritual and political landscape of Tibet and the world. In this detailed exploration, we will delve into Tenzin Gyatso's early life, his spiritual journey, his leadership of the Tibetan people, his global impact, and his enduring legacy.

Early Life and Education

Tenzin Gyatso was born to a farming family in the remote Himalayan region of Tibet. At the age of two, he was identified as the reincarnation of the 13th Dalai Lama, Thubten Gyatso, through a series of tests and omens conducted by Tibetan Buddhist monks. He was enthroned as the spiritual leader of Tibet and began his education in Buddhist philosophy, scripture, and meditation under the guidance of esteemed teachers.

Despite his young age, Tenzin Gyatso showed remarkable intelligence, wisdom, and compassion. He displayed a deep understanding of Buddhist teachings and a natural inclination towards meditation and contemplation. As he grew older, he continued to devote himself to his spiritual practice and to the welfare of the Tibetan people.

Political Turmoil and Exile

In 1950, when Tenzin Gyatso was just 15 years old, Tibet came under Chinese control following the invasion by the People's Liberation Army. The Dalai Lama assumed political leadership at the age of 16 in the midst of escalating tensions between Tibet and China. In 1959, following a failed uprising against Chinese rule, Tenzin

Gyatso was forced to flee Tibet and seek asylum in India, where he has resided in exile ever since.

The Chinese government's occupation of Tibet led to widespread human rights abuses, religious persecution, and cultural repression. Tenzin Gyatso has been a vocal advocate for the rights of the Tibetan people, calling for autonomy and freedom for Tibet and denouncing China's policies of assimilation and control.

Spiritual Leadership and Teachings

As the spiritual leader of Tibetan Buddhism, Tenzin Gyatso has dedicated his life to promoting peace, compassion, and nonviolence. He has traveled the world, giving teachings, lectures, and public talks on Buddhist philosophy, ethics, and mindfulness. His message of universal responsibility, interdependence, and the importance of inner peace has resonated with people of all faiths and backgrounds.

Tenzin Gyatso's teachings emphasize the importance of cultivating compassion, wisdom, and altruism in order to alleviate suffering and create a more harmonious and compassionate world. He has written numerous books on Buddhist philosophy and practice, including "The Art of Happiness" and "The Book of Joy," co-authored with Archbishop Desmond Tutu.

Nobel Peace Prize

In 1989, Tenzin Gyatso was awarded the Nobel Peace Prize in recognition of his nonviolent struggle for the liberation of Tibet and his efforts to promote peace and human rights on a global scale. He was the first Nobel laureate to be recognized for his work in the field of spirituality and religion.

In his acceptance speech, Tenzin Gyatso emphasized the importance of compassion, dialogue, and reconciliation in resolving conflicts and building a more peaceful and just world. He called for greater respect for human rights, religious freedom, and cultural diversity, urging people to overcome divisions and work together for the common good.

Dialogue with Science

Tenzin Gyatso has long been interested in fostering dialogue between Buddhism and modern science, recognizing the potential for mutual enrichment and understanding. He has engaged in conversations with leading scientists, philosophers, and scholars on topics such as consciousness, ethics, and the nature of reality.

Through initiatives such as the Mind and Life Institute, founded in 1987, Tenzin Gyatso has facilitated dialogue and collaboration between Buddhist practitioners and scientists, exploring the intersections between contemplative practices and empirical research. He has contributed to scientific understanding of the mind, consciousness, and human well-being, while also drawing on scientific insights to inform Buddhist teachings and practices.

Environmental Advocacy

Tenzin Gyatso is also a passionate advocate for environmental sustainability and conservation. He has spoken out on issues such as climate change, deforestation, and biodiversity loss, highlighting the interconnectedness of all living beings and the importance of protecting the natural world.

In 1989, Tenzin Gyatso launched the Five Point Peace Plan for Tibet, which outlined proposals for resolving the conflict between Tibet and China through nonviolent means. The plan called for the demilitarization of Tibet, the protection of its natural environment, and the promotion of human rights and democracy.

Global Influence and Legacy

Tenzin Gyatso's influence extends far beyond the borders of Tibet and the Buddhist community. He is revered as a spiritual leader and moral authority by millions of people around the world, regardless of their religious or cultural background. His teachings on compassion, ethics, and mindfulness have inspired countless individuals to lead more meaningful and compassionate lives.

The Dalai Lama's commitment to peace, nonviolence, and dialogue has earned him respect and admiration from world leaders, religious figures, and ordinary people alike. His tireless efforts to promote human rights, environmental sustainability, and interfaith harmony have made him a beloved and revered figure on the global stage.

Conclusion

In conclusion, Tenzin Gyatso, the 14th Dalai Lama, is a figure of immense spiritual significance and moral authority whose life and teachings have touched the hearts and minds of people around the world. From his early years in Tibet to his exile in India and his global travels as a spiritual leader and advocate for peace, the Dalai Lama has remained steadfast in his commitment to the well-being of humanity and the planet. His message of compassion, nonviolence, and interdependence resonates deeply in an increasingly interconnected and troubled world, offering hope and guidance to those who seek a path of wisdom and understanding. As the Dalai Lama continues his journey of service and enlightenment, his legacy will endure as a beacon of light and inspiration for generations to come, reminding us of the transformative power of love, kindness, and inner peace.

Chapter 14: Babar Ali

Babar Ali, often referred to as the "Youngest Headmaster in the World," is a remarkable individual who has made significant contributions to education and social change in his community. Born on March 18, 1993, in Murshidabad, West Bengal, India, Babar Ali's journey from a young boy with a passion for learning to a pioneering educator and advocate for children's rights is both inspiring and uplifting. In this detailed exploration, we will delve into Babar Ali's early life, his innovative approach to education, his impact on his community, and his ongoing efforts to create positive change.

Early Life and Inspiration

Babar Ali was born into a humble family in a small village in West Bengal. Despite limited resources and opportunities, Babar's parents instilled in him a deep appreciation for education and learning. From a young age, Babar was eager to pursue knowledge and make a difference in the lives of those around him.

Inspired by his father, who was a primary school teacher, Babar began teaching his younger sister and other children in his village at the age of nine. He transformed a small, dilapidated shed into a makeshift school, using chalk and a blackboard to impart lessons in basic literacy and numeracy.

Founding of Anand Shiksha Niketan

In 2002, at the age of 11, Babar Ali founded Anand Shiksha Niketan (ASN), a free school for underprivileged children in his village. With the support of his family and community members, Babar converted a portion of his family's ancestral land into a school building, complete with classrooms, a library, and a playground.

ASN provided children from low-income families with access to quality education and holistic development opportunities. Babar recruited volunteer teachers from the local community to help teach subjects such as mathematics, science, English, and social studies. He also organized extracurricular activities, including sports, arts, and cultural events, to enrich the students' learning experience.

Innovative Teaching Methods

Babar Ali's approach to education was innovative and student-centered. He recognized the importance of engaging students in active learning and fostering their curiosity and creativity. In addition to traditional classroom instruction, Babar incorporated interactive teaching methods, group activities, and hands-on learning experiences to make education enjoyable and meaningful for his students.

He also leveraged technology and multimedia resources to enhance the learning process, using educational videos, computer-based tutorials, and interactive games to supplement classroom instruction. Babar's dedication to providing a holistic and empowering education to his students earned him praise and recognition from educators and policymakers around the world.

Recognition and Awards

Babar Ali's extraordinary achievements as a young educator garnered widespread attention and acclaim. He received numerous awards and honors for his contributions to education and social change, including the National Award for Bravery from the Government of India in 2006.

In 2009, Babar Ali was invited to deliver a TED Talk titled "Babar Ali: India's Youngest Headmaster," where he shared his inspiring story and vision for education. The TED Talk went viral, reaching millions of viewers worldwide and further amplifying Babar's message of hope and empowerment.

Impact on the Community

Through his work with Anand Shiksha Niketan, Babar Ali has had a profound impact on his community and beyond. The school has provided educational opportunities to hundreds of children from marginalized backgrounds, empowering them to break the cycle of poverty and achieve their full potential.

Many of Babar's former students have gone on to pursue higher education and successful careers, becoming role models and leaders in their communities. ASN has also inspired similar initiatives in other parts of India and around the world, demonstrating the transformative power of grassroots education and community-driven development.

Challenges and Resilience

Despite his success, Babar Ali has faced numerous challenges and obstacles along the way. Funding shortages, bureaucratic hurdles, and societal prejudices have posed significant barriers to the growth and sustainability of ASN. However, Babar has remained resilient and determined in the face of adversity, rallying support from donors, volunteers, and government officials to keep the school running.

Ongoing Efforts and Future Plans

Babar Ali continues to be actively involved in the operations and expansion of Anand Shiksha Niketan. He is committed to providing quality education to even more children in his community and improving the school's infrastructure and facilities. Babar also advocates for policy reforms and investments in education at the local, national, and international levels, calling for greater access to quality education for all children, regardless of their background or circumstances.

Legacy and Inspiration

Babar Ali's legacy extends far beyond the walls of Anand Shiksha Niketan. He is a symbol of hope, resilience, and the transformative power of education to create positive change in the world. Babar's story has inspired millions of people around the world to believe in the power of one individual to make a difference and to take action to address the root causes of poverty, inequality, and injustice.

Conclusion

In conclusion, Babar Ali's journey from a young boy with a dream to a pioneering educator and advocate for children's rights is a testament to the power of determination, passion, and compassion to transform lives and communities. Through his visionary leadership and tireless dedication, Babar has not only provided educational opportunities to hundreds of children but has also inspired a global movement for social change and educational equity. As he continues his mission to build a brighter future for the next generation, Babar Ali serves as a beacon of hope and inspiration for us all.

Chapter 15: Tilly Lockey

Tilly Lockey is an extraordinary individual whose story is one of resilience, determination, and inspiration. Born on May 12, 2005, in Consett, County Durham, England, Tilly's life took a dramatic turn at the age of 15 months when she contracted meningococcal septicaemia, a severe form of bacterial meningitis. As a result of the illness, Tilly had to undergo a double hand amputation and the partial amputation of both legs. Despite facing immense challenges, Tilly has emerged as a beacon of hope and a symbol of courage, using her experiences to advocate for others and drive positive change in the world. In this detailed exploration, we will delve into Tilly Lockey's early life, her journey of adaptation and resilience, her advocacy work, and her impact on the global community.

Early Life and Illness

Tilly Lockey's early life was like that of any other child, filled with laughter, curiosity, and endless possibilities. However, at the age of 15 months, her world was turned upside down when she fell seriously ill with meningococcal septicaemia. The illness progressed rapidly, causing widespread damage to Tilly's body and ultimately resulting in the loss of her hands and the partial amputation of her legs.

The aftermath of the illness was a challenging time for Tilly and her family as they navigated the physical, emotional, and psychological effects of her condition. Adjusting to life without hands presented numerous obstacles and uncertainties, but Tilly's spirit remained unbroken, and she faced each new challenge with courage and determination.

Adaptation and Rehabilitation

In the years following her illness, Tilly Lockey underwent extensive rehabilitation and adaptation to her new way of life. With the support of her family, healthcare professionals, and prosthetics experts, Tilly learned to use prosthetic limbs to perform everyday tasks and regain her independence.

Through sheer determination and perseverance, Tilly mastered the use of her prosthetic hands, learning to write, eat, dress, and engage in activities that many take for granted. She embraced her prosthetic limbs as extensions of herself, finding creative ways to adapt and thrive in a world designed for able-bodied individuals.

Advocacy and Awareness

As Tilly Lockey grew older, she became increasingly passionate about using her experiences to make a difference in the lives of others. She recognized the importance of raising awareness about meningitis and the impact it can have on individuals and families, and she became a vocal advocate for meningitis awareness and prevention.

Tilly also became an advocate for disability rights and inclusion, speaking out against discrimination and advocating for equal opportunities for people with disabilities. Through public speaking engagements, media appearances, and social media activism, she has raised awareness about the challenges faced by people with disabilities and championed the importance of accessibility and inclusivity in all aspects of society.

Technology and Innovation

One of the most remarkable aspects of Tilly Lockey's journey is her embrace of technology and innovation to overcome her physical limitations. Tilly has become a pioneer in the field of bionic prosthetics, working with leading researchers and engineers to develop and test cutting-edge prosthetic technologies.

In 2018, Tilly became one of the youngest recipients of a bionic hand from Open Bionics, a company specializing in affordable, 3D-printed bionic limbs. The bionic hand, which is controlled by muscle signals in Tilly's residual limbs, has transformed her life, giving her greater dexterity, functionality, and independence.

Inspirational Figure and Role Model

Tilly Lockey's journey of adaptation and resilience has made her an inspirational figure and role model for people of all ages and backgrounds. Her courage, determination, and positive outlook on life serve as a source of inspiration for those facing adversity and challenges of their own.

Through her advocacy work, Tilly has empowered countless individuals to embrace their differences, overcome obstacles, and pursue their dreams. She has shown that disability does not define a person's capabilities or limit their potential, and that with the right support and mindset, anything is possible.

Impact on the Global Community

Tilly Lockey's impact extends far beyond her local community in County Durham, England. Through her advocacy efforts and media presence, she has reached millions of people around the world, spreading messages of hope, resilience, and inclusivity.

Her story has been featured in numerous media outlets, including television programs, documentaries, and online platforms, amplifying her message of empowerment and inspiring others to make a positive difference in the world. Tilly's advocacy work has also led to increased awareness and support for meningitis research and prevention efforts, saving lives and preventing needless suffering.

Future Plans and Aspirations

As Tilly Lockey continues her journey, she remains committed to making a positive impact in the world and advocating for change. She plans to continue her work in disability rights and inclusion, using her platform to amplify the voices of marginalized communities and drive systemic change.

Tilly also hopes to inspire future generations of young people to embrace their uniqueness and pursue their passions, regardless of the obstacles they may face. She dreams of a world where everyone is treated with dignity, respect, and compassion, and where disability is seen not as a barrier, but as a source of strength and resilience.

Conclusion

In conclusion, Tilly Lockey's story is a testament to the power of resilience, determination, and hope in the face of adversity. Despite facing immense challenges at a young age, Tilly has emerged as a powerful advocate for meningitis awareness, disability rights, and inclusivity.

Her journey of adaptation and empowerment serves as a source of inspiration for people around the world, reminding us all of the importance of embracing our differences, overcoming obstacles, and championing equality and justice for all. Tilly Lockey's impact on the global community is profound and enduring, and her legacy will continue to inspire generations to come.

Chapter 16: William Kamkwamba

William Kamkwamba is a name synonymous with ingenuity, perseverance, and the power of education to transform lives. Born on August 5, 1987, in a small village called Wimbe in Malawi, William's story is one of extraordinary determination and resourcefulness in the face of adversity. From humble beginnings to international acclaim, William Kamkwamba's journey is a testament to the human spirit and the ability to overcome seemingly insurmountable obstacles through innovation and education.

Early Life and Inspiration

Growing up in rural Malawi, William Kamkwamba experienced firsthand the challenges of poverty, hunger, and limited access to education. Despite these obstacles, William had an insatiable curiosity and a passion for learning, fueled by his love of books and his natural inclination towards tinkering and experimentation.

At the age of 14, William was forced to drop out of school due to his family's inability to afford the tuition fees. Determined to continue his education and make a difference in his community, William turned to the local library, where he devoured books on science, technology, and engineering, teaching himself the principles of physics, electricity, and mechanics.

The Windmill Project

Inspired by a book he found in the library called "Using Energy," William Kamkwamba embarked on a remarkable project to build a windmill to generate electricity for his village. Despite having no formal training or access to advanced tools and materials, William used his ingenuity and resourcefulness to scavenge parts and materials from scrap yards, junkyards, and local markets.

Using bicycle parts, PVC pipes, old tractor fans, and other salvaged materials, William constructed a makeshift windmill on his family's farm. With the help of his friends and family, he erected the windmill, which stood tall at over 16 feet and had blades made from plastic pipes and sheet metal.

Impact and Recognition

In 2007, William Kamkwamba's homemade windmill attracted international attention when journalist Bryan Mealer and photographer Mike Hettwer stumbled upon his story while visiting Malawi. They were amazed by William's ingenuity and determination and decided to share his story with the world.

The story of William's windmill spread like wildfire, capturing the imaginations of people around the globe and earning him widespread acclaim and recognition. William was invited to speak at prestigious events such as the TEDGlobal conference in Arusha, Tanzania, where he delivered a moving talk titled "How I Harnessed the Wind" that garnered millions of views online.

Education and Empowerment

William Kamkwamba's windmill project not only provided electricity to his village but also inspired a new generation of young Africans to pursue education and innovation. His story highlighted the importance of access to education and resources in empowering individuals to create positive change in their communities.

With the support of donors and well-wishers from around the world, William was able to resume his education and attend secondary school. He later went on to study at the African Leadership Academy in South Africa and Dartmouth College in the United States, where he pursued his passion for science, technology, and engineering.

Beyond the Windmill

Since gaining international recognition, William Kamkwamba has continued to use his platform to advocate for education, renewable energy, and sustainable development in Africa and beyond. He has traveled the world, sharing his story and inspiring audiences with his message of hope, resilience, and innovation.

In addition to his advocacy work, William has collaborated with organizations and institutions to promote access to clean energy technologies and educational opportunities in rural communities. He has also written a memoir titled "The Boy Who Harnessed the Wind," which chronicles his remarkable journey from a young boy with a dream to an international symbol of hope and inspiration.

Legacy and Impact

William Kamkwamba's legacy extends far beyond the windmill that he built in his village. His story has inspired millions of people around the world to believe in the power of education, innovation, and perseverance to overcome adversity and create positive change.

Through his work as an author, speaker, and advocate, William continues to inspire young people to pursue their passions, follow their dreams, and make a difference in the world. His story serves as a reminder that no obstacle is insurmountable and that with determination, creativity, and hard work, anything is possible.

Conclusion

In conclusion, William Kamkwamba's journey from a small village in Malawi to international acclaim is a testament to the transformative power of education, innovation, and perseverance. His story has touched the hearts and minds of people around the world, inspiring millions to believe in their ability to create positive change in their communities and beyond.

William Kamkwamba's windmill stands not only as a symbol of renewable energy and sustainability but also as a beacon of hope and resilience for generations to come. His legacy will continue to inspire and empower individuals to harness their ingenuity and creativity to tackle the challenges of our time and build a brighter, more sustainable future for all.

Chapter 17: Asha Gond

Asha Gond, often known as "The Water Warrior," is a remarkable environmental activist and community leader from the village of Mangthar in the Rajnandgaon district of Chhattisgarh, India. Her story is one of courage, resilience, and determination in the face of environmental degradation and water scarcity. Born into a tribal family, Asha Gond has dedicated her life to fighting for the rights of indigenous communities and the protection of natural resources. In this detailed exploration, we will delve into Asha Gond's background, her activism, her impact on her community, and her ongoing efforts to create positive change.

Early Life and Background

Asha Gond was born and raised in Mangthar, a small village in the tribal heartland of Chhattisgarh. Growing up, she witnessed firsthand the environmental degradation and water scarcity plaguing her community. Rivers and streams were drying up, forests were disappearing, and traditional sources of livelihood were under threat.

Despite these challenges, Asha was determined to make a difference. From a young age, she showed a keen interest in environmental conservation and community development, inspired by the teachings of her elders and the deep spiritual connection to nature ingrained in tribal culture.

Fight for Clean Water

One of the most pressing issues facing Asha Gond's community was access to clean and safe drinking water. Like many rural areas in India, Mangthar struggled with water scarcity, exacerbated by deforestation, pollution, and erratic rainfall patterns. Women and girls were often forced to walk long distances to fetch water from distant sources, putting their health and safety at risk.

Determined to address this critical issue, Asha mobilized her community to take action. She organized meetings, rallies, and awareness campaigns to raise awareness about the importance of water conservation and sanitation. She also lobbied local authorities and government officials to invest in water infrastructure and improve access to clean water for marginalized communities.

Rainwater Harvesting and Traditional Wisdom

One of the innovative solutions championed by Asha Gond is rainwater harvesting, a traditional practice that has been used for centuries by indigenous communities in India. Recognizing the importance of harnessing rainwater to replenish groundwater reserves and mitigate the effects of drought, Asha led efforts to promote rainwater harvesting techniques in her village.

With the help of local volunteers and NGOs, Asha organized workshops and training sessions to teach community members how to build and maintain rainwater harvesting structures such as rooftop rainwater tanks, check dams, and percolation pits. These initiatives not only helped to improve access to water but also empowered communities to become more self-reliant and resilient in the face of climate change.

Environmental Conservation and Reforestation

In addition to her work on water issues, Asha Gond has been a vocal advocate for environmental conservation and reforestation. She recognized the importance of protecting forests and biodiversity as essential components of sustainable development and community resilience.

Asha mobilized her community to participate in tree planting drives, forest conservation initiatives, and wildlife protection efforts. She also worked closely with local forest departments and conservation organizations to implement sustainable land management practices and promote eco-friendly livelihoods such as agroforestry and beekeeping.

Empowerment of Women and Youth

Asha Gond is a strong proponent of women's rights and gender equality. She believes that empowering women and girls is essential for building strong and resilient communities. Through her activism, Asha has worked to break down gender barriers and empower women to take on leadership roles in environmental conservation and community development.

She has organized women's self-help groups, vocational training programs, and skill development workshops to provide women with the tools and resources they need to become agents of change in their communities. Asha has also been a mentor and role model for young girls, inspiring them to pursue education, activism, and careers in fields traditionally dominated by men.

Recognition and Awards

Asha Gond's tireless efforts to protect the environment and improve the lives of her community members have earned her widespread recognition and acclaim. She has received numerous awards and honors for her contributions to environmental conservation and social justice, including the prestigious "Water Warrior Award" from the Government of India.

In 2017, Asha was invited to participate in the United Nations Climate Change Conference (COP23) in Bonn, Germany, where she shared her experiences and insights on grassroots environmental activism and community resilience. Her participation in international forums has helped to amplify the voices of indigenous communities and raise awareness about the urgent need for action on climate change and environmental justice.

Challenges and Resilience

Despite her many achievements, Asha Gond has faced numerous challenges and obstacles in her activism. She has encountered resistance from vested interests, bureaucratic hurdles, and cultural barriers that have sought to undermine her efforts and suppress her voice.

However, Asha's resilience and determination have enabled her to overcome these challenges and continue her fight for environmental justice. She remains undeterred in her commitment to protecting the environment and empowering marginalized communities, drawing strength from the support of her fellow activists and the resilience of nature itself.

Ongoing Efforts and Future Plans

Asha Gond's work is far from over. She continues to be actively involved in grassroots activism and community development initiatives in her village and beyond. She is working to expand access to clean water, promote sustainable agriculture, and strengthen environmental governance systems at the local and national levels.

Asha also plans to continue advocating for the rights of indigenous peoples and marginalized communities, highlighting their unique knowledge, cultures, and contributions to environmental conservation. She hopes to inspire a new generation of environmental leaders and activists to carry on the torch of activism and create a more just, equitable, and sustainable world for all.

Conclusion

In conclusion, Asha Gond's story is a powerful reminder of the transformative impact that one individual can have on their community and the world. Her dedication to environmental conservation, social justice, and community empowerment serves as an inspiration to us all.

Through her activism and advocacy, Asha Gond has shown that grassroots movements and community-based solutions are essential for addressing complex challenges such as climate change, water scarcity, and environmental degradation. Her tireless efforts have not only improved the lives of her fellow community members but have also inspired people around the world to take action and make a positive difference in their own communities.

As we face the pressing challenges of the 21st century, Asha Gond's example reminds us of the power of resilience, determination, and collective action to create a more sustainable and equitable future for generations to come.

Chapter 18: Lizzie Velasquez

Elizabeth Anne Velásquez, commonly known as Lizzie Velasquez, is a motivational speaker, author, and social media personality who has become an advocate for self-love, anti-bullying, and disability rights. Born on March 13, 1989, in Austin, Texas, Lizzie's life took an unexpected turn when she was diagnosed with two rare conditions: Marfanoid-progeroid-lipodystrophy syndrome, a genetic disorder that prevents her from gaining weight, and neonatal progeroid syndrome, a condition that affects her appearance and physical health. Despite facing countless challenges and cruel bullying throughout her life, Lizzie has emerged as a powerful voice for positivity, resilience, and embracing one's uniqueness. In this detailed exploration, we will delve into Lizzie Velasquez's early life, her experiences with bullying, her rise to prominence as a motivational speaker, her advocacy work, and her impact on the world.

Early Life and Diagnosis

Lizzie Velasquez was born premature and weighed just 2 pounds, 10 ounces at birth. Doctors soon realized that something was different about Lizzie, but it wasn't until she was four years old that she was diagnosed with Marfanoid-progeroid-lipodystrophy syndrome, a condition so rare that she is one of only three people in the world known to have it.

Growing up, Lizzie faced numerous health challenges related to her condition, including vision problems, joint pain, and a weakened immune system. She was frequently hospitalized and underwent numerous medical procedures, but her resilience and positive outlook on life never wavered.

Bullying and Adversity

One of the most difficult aspects of Lizzie Velasquez's childhood was the relentless bullying and taunting she endured from her peers.

From a young age, Lizzie was subjected to cruel insults, stares, and exclusion because of her appearance and physical differences.

Despite the hurtful words and actions of others, Lizzie refused to let the bullies define her or dictate her self-worth. With the unwavering support of her family and friends, she found the strength to rise above the negativity and embrace her uniqueness.

Rise to Prominence

Lizzie Velasquez first gained widespread attention in 2006, when she discovered a YouTube video titled "The World's Ugliest Woman" that had been uploaded by an anonymous user. To her horror, she realized that the video was about her, featuring images taken from her social media profiles and accompanied by hurtful comments and derogatory remarks.

Rather than succumbing to despair, Lizzie decided to turn the negative experience into an opportunity to spread a message of love, acceptance, and empowerment. She began speaking out against cyberbullying and promoting self-love and body positivity through her own social media channels.

Motivational Speaking and Advocacy

As Lizzie Velasquez's story gained traction online, she was invited to share her experiences and insights at schools, conferences, and events around the world. Her powerful message of resilience, forgiveness, and compassion resonated with audiences of all ages and backgrounds, inspiring countless individuals to embrace their uniqueness and stand up against bullying.

In addition to her work as a motivational speaker, Lizzie has become a passionate advocate for anti-bullying legislation and disability rights. She has testified before Congress, spoken at the United Nations, and collaborated with lawmakers and policymakers to enact meaningful change and promote inclusivity and equality for all.

Authorship and Media Appearances

Lizzie Velasquez has written several books chronicling her life experiences and sharing her wisdom and advice with others. Her memoir, "Lizzie Beautiful: The Lizzie Velasquez Story," was published in 2010 and became a bestseller, further amplifying her message of resilience and self-acceptance.

Lizzie has also been featured in numerous media outlets, including television programs, documentaries, and news articles. She has appeared on shows such as "The Today Show," "The View," and "Good Morning America," sharing her story and advocating for positive change in society.

Social Media Influence

One of the most powerful tools in Lizzie Velasquez's advocacy arsenal is social media. Through platforms like YouTube, Instagram, and Twitter, she has built a large and engaged following, using her platforms to spread messages of positivity, kindness, and inclusivity.

Lizzie's social media presence has allowed her to connect with people from all over the world and to share her story with a global audience. She regularly posts inspirational messages, personal reflections, and behind-the-scenes glimpses of her life, fostering a sense of community and support among her followers.

Legacy and Impact

Lizzie Velasquez's impact on the world is immeasurable. Through her resilience, courage, and unwavering commitment to kindness, she has inspired millions of people to embrace their uniqueness, stand up against bullying, and cultivate a culture of compassion and acceptance.

Her advocacy work has led to tangible changes in policies and attitudes towards disability rights and anti-bullying initiatives, helping to create a more inclusive and equitable society for all. Her message of love, forgiveness, and self-empowerment continues to resonate with people of all ages and backgrounds, reminding us of the power of kindness to heal wounds and unite communities.

Conclusion

In conclusion, Lizzie Velasquez's journey from a bullied teenager to a global advocate for kindness and inclusivity is a testament to the resilience of the human spirit. Despite facing countless challenges and adversities, she has emerged as a beacon of hope and inspiration for millions of people around the world.

Through her advocacy work, motivational speaking, and social media presence, Lizzie Velasquez has touched the lives of countless individuals, spreading a message of love, acceptance, and empowerment wherever she goes. Her legacy will continue to inspire future generations to stand up against bullying, embrace their uniqueness, and make the world a kinder and more compassionate place for all.

Chapter 19: Laxmi Agarwal

Laxmi Agarwal is an Indian acid attack survivor, activist, and campaigner for the rights of acid attack victims. Her story is one of resilience, courage, and the fight against gender-based violence. Born on June 1, 1990, in New Delhi, India, Laxmi's life was forever changed at the age of 15 when she became the victim of a brutal acid attack perpetrated by a man whose advances she had rejected. Despite the trauma and physical disfigurement she endured, Laxmi refused to be defined by her scars and instead chose to use her experience to advocate for change and raise awareness about the issue of acid attacks in India. In this detailed exploration, we will delve into Laxmi Agarwal's early life, the horrific acid attack she survived, her journey of recovery and activism, and her impact on the fight against acid violence and gender-based discrimination.

Early Life and Background

Laxmi Agarwal was born and raised in a middle-class family in New Delhi, India. She had dreams and aspirations like any other teenager, but her life took a tragic turn when she became the victim of an acid attack at the tender age of 15. The attack, orchestrated by a man more than twice her age, was a result of Laxmi's refusal to reciprocate his romantic advances.

The Acid Attack

On a fateful day in 2005, Laxmi Agarwal's life was forever changed when she was attacked with acid while she was waiting at a bus stop in New Delhi. The assailant, a 32-year-old man whose advances Laxmi had rejected, poured acid on her face as an act of revenge. The attack left Laxmi with severe burns and disfigurement, causing her excruciating pain and lifelong physical and emotional scars.

Journey of Recovery and Resilience

In the aftermath of the attack, Laxmi Agarwal faced numerous challenges as she struggled to come to terms with her new reality.

She underwent multiple surgeries and extensive medical treatments to repair the damage caused by the acid, but the scars remained both physically and emotionally.

Despite the trauma and pain she endured, Laxmi refused to let the attack define her or diminish her spirit. With the support of her family and loved ones, she embarked on a journey of recovery and resilience, determined to reclaim her life and make a positive impact in the world.

Advocacy and Activism

Inspired by her own experience and fueled by a desire to prevent others from suffering the same fate, Laxmi Agarwal became a powerful voice for change and an advocate for the rights of acid attack survivors. She began speaking out against acid violence and gender-based discrimination, sharing her story with the world and calling for justice and accountability for the perpetrators of such heinous crimes.

Laxmi's advocacy efforts gained momentum when she filed a Public Interest Litigation (PIL) in the Supreme Court of India seeking regulation of the sale of acid and rehabilitation and compensation for acid attack survivors. Her petition led to the landmark Supreme Court judgment in 2013, which imposed restrictions on the sale of acid and provided legal recognition and support for acid attack survivors.

Rise to Prominence

Laxmi Agarwal's courage and determination captured the attention of the media and the public, catapulting her to national and international prominence. She became a symbol of resilience and empowerment, appearing on television programs, documentaries, and talk shows to share her story and advocate for change.

In 2014, Laxmi was honored with the International Women of Courage Award by the U.S. Department of State for her fearless advocacy and relentless efforts to combat acid violence and empower survivors. She was also named one of BBC's 100 Women in recognition of her inspiring leadership and activism.

Impact and Legacy

Laxmi Agarwal's advocacy and activism have had a profound impact on the fight against acid violence and gender-based discrimination in India and beyond. Her efforts have helped to raise awareness about the issue of acid attacks and to push for legal and policy reforms to prevent such crimes and support survivors.

Through her organization, the Laxmi Agarwal Foundation, she provides support and assistance to acid attack survivors, including medical treatment, counseling, vocational training, and legal aid. She also works to change societal attitudes and perceptions towards survivors, challenging stigma and promoting inclusion and acceptance.

Challenges and Triumphs

Despite her many achievements, Laxmi Agarwal continues to face challenges in her advocacy work, including resistance from conservative elements in society, bureaucratic hurdles, and the slow pace of legal reforms. However, she remains undeterred in her commitment to the cause and continues to fight tirelessly for justice and equality for all.

Laxmi's triumphs are not just her own but also those of the countless survivors whose voices she amplifies and whose rights she champions. Through her courage, resilience, and unwavering determination, she has inspired a new generation of activists and advocates to join the fight against gender-based violence and to work towards a more just and equitable society.

Personal Life and Inspiration

In addition to her activism, Laxmi Agarwal is also a loving mother and wife. She draws strength and inspiration from her family and her faith, which sustain her in the face of adversity and fuel her passion for justice and compassion.

Laxmi's journey is a testament to the power of resilience, courage, and determination to overcome even the most unimaginable challenges. Her story serves as a beacon of hope and inspiration for survivors of violence everywhere, reminding us all of the importance of speaking out against injustice and standing up for what is right.

Conclusion

In conclusion, Laxmi Agarwal's journey from an acid attack survivor to a fearless advocate for change is a testament to the strength of the human spirit and the power of resilience and determination to overcome adversity. Her courage, advocacy, and activism have helped to raise awareness about the issue of acid violence and to push for legal and policy reforms to prevent such crimes and support survivors.

Laxmi's impact extends far beyond her own story, inspiring countless individuals to stand up against gender-based violence and to work towards a more just and equitable society. Her legacy will continue to inspire future generations to speak out against injustice and to fight for the rights and dignity of all people, regardless of their gender, race, or background.

Chapter 20: Madison Steiner

Madison Steiner, also known by her nickname "Peach," is an inspiring philanthropist and artist who has made a significant impact through her creative and compassionate endeavors. She is best known for her non-profit organization, Peach's Neet Feet, which she founded to provide hand-painted shoes to children battling serious illnesses and disabilities. Her journey is one of compassion, creativity, and a relentless commitment to bringing joy and hope to those in need. This detailed exploration will delve into Madison Steiner's background, her motivations, the inception and growth of Peach's Neet Feet, her impact on the community, and her ongoing efforts and future aspirations.

Early Life and Background

Madison Steiner was born in North Dakota and raised in a close-knit family that emphasized the importance of kindness, creativity, and helping others. From a young age, Madison displayed a natural talent for art and a deep sense of empathy for those around her. These qualities would later become the foundation of her life's work.

Madison attended college in New Mexico, where she continued to cultivate her artistic skills while also working various jobs. It was during this period that her desire to make a tangible difference in the lives of children facing serious health challenges began to take shape.

The Birth of Peach's Neet Feet

The inception of Peach's Neet Feet (PNF) can be traced back to 2011. Madison Steiner, affectionately known as "Peach" by her friends and family, combined her artistic talent with her passion for helping others to create something truly unique. The idea was simple yet powerful: to hand-paint custom shoes for children battling cancer, chronic illnesses, and disabilities.

Madison began by painting shoes in her spare time and donating them to children in hospitals. Each pair of shoes was personalized to reflect the child's interests, favorite colors, and unique personality. This personal touch made each gift not just a pair of shoes, but a symbol of love, hope, and individuality.

Growth and Expansion

What started as a small, personal project quickly gained momentum as word spread about Madison's heartfelt initiative. Families, healthcare professionals, and communities were deeply moved by the joy and positivity that the custom-painted shoes brought to the children. As demand for the shoes grew, Madison realized that she needed to expand her efforts to reach more children.

In 2012, Madison officially founded Peach's Neet Feet as a non-profit organization. She began recruiting volunteers, known as "Peach Painters," who shared her passion for art and helping children. These volunteers helped paint shoes, allowing the organization to fulfill more requests and reach a wider audience.

Impact on the Community

Peach's Neet Feet quickly became more than just an organization; it became a movement. The hand-painted shoes provided by PNF did more than just cover children's feet—they lifted their spirits, boosted their self-esteem, and reminded them that they were loved and supported. Each pair of shoes told a story and helped to create a connection between the child and the artist.

One of the most significant aspects of PNF's impact is the personal connection it fosters. Madison and her team make an effort to get to know each child's story, interests, and preferences before creating their custom shoes. This personal touch ensures that each pair is a true reflection of the child's personality and brings a sense of normalcy and joy into their lives during challenging times.

Stories of Hope and Resilience

The stories of the children who have received shoes from Peach's Neet Feet are testimonies to the profound impact of Madison Steiner's work. Each story is unique, but they all share a common theme: the power of kindness and creativity to bring hope and healing.

For example, there's the story of a young girl named Emma who was battling leukemia. Emma loved butterflies, and Madison created a pair of shoes adorned with beautiful, vibrant butterflies. The shoes became a symbol of hope and transformation for Emma, and they lifted her spirits during her treatment.

Another story is that of a boy named Jack who was diagnosed with cerebral palsy. Jack was a huge fan of superheroes, and Madison designed a pair of shoes featuring his favorite characters. The shoes not only brought a smile to Jack's face but also made him feel empowered and strong, like the superheroes he admired.

Challenges and Triumphs

Running a non-profit organization, especially one as unique as Peach's Neet Feet, comes with its own set of challenges. Madison Steiner has faced numerous obstacles, including securing funding, managing logistics, and balancing the growing demands of the organization with her personal life.

Despite these challenges, Madison's unwavering commitment to her mission has led to numerous triumphs. Peach's Neet Feet has grown exponentially since its inception, receiving support from individuals, businesses, and communities across the country. The organization has been able to provide thousands of pairs of custom-painted shoes to children in need, each one bringing joy and hope to its recipient.

Recognition and Awards

Madison Steiner's dedication and impact have not gone unnoticed. She has received numerous awards and accolades for her work with Peach's Neet Feet. In 2013, she was honored with the Muhammad Ali Humanitarian Award for her selfless contributions to society. This prestigious award, named after the legendary boxer and humanitarian, recognizes individuals who have made significant efforts to improve the lives of others.

Madison has also been featured in various media outlets, including television programs, magazines, and online publications. Her story has inspired countless individuals to take action in their own communities and to use their talents to make a difference.

Ongoing Efforts and Future Aspirations

As Peach's Neet Feet continues to grow, Madison Steiner remains focused on expanding the organization's reach and impact. She is constantly seeking new ways to support and uplift children facing serious health challenges and to promote kindness and empathy in society.

One of Madison's ongoing efforts is to establish partnerships with hospitals, clinics, and other healthcare organizations to ensure that more children can benefit from the joy and hope that Peach's Neet Feet provides. She is also working to develop new programs and initiatives that complement the core mission of the organization, such as art therapy workshops and support networks for families.

In addition to her work with Peach's Neet Feet, Madison is passionate about inspiring others to embrace their creativity and to use their talents for good. She frequently speaks at schools, conferences, and community events, sharing her story and encouraging others to make a positive impact in their own way.

Legacy and Impact

Madison Steiner's legacy is one of compassion, creativity, and unwavering dedication to making the world a better place. Through Peach's Neet Feet, she has touched the lives of thousands of children and families, bringing light and hope to those facing some of life's most difficult challenges.

Her work has also had a ripple effect, inspiring a global community of volunteers, supporters, and advocates who are committed to spreading kindness and making a difference. Madison's story is a powerful reminder of the impact that one person can have when they combine their passion with a genuine desire to help others.

Conclusion

In conclusion, Madison Steiner's journey from a young artist with a dream to the founder of Peach's Neet Feet is a testament to the power of creativity, kindness, and resilience. Her unwavering commitment to bringing joy and hope to children battling serious illnesses and disabilities has made a profound impact on countless lives.

Through her work with Peach's Neet Feet, Madison has shown that even the simplest acts of kindness can have a transformative effect. Her story is an inspiration to us all, reminding us of the importance of empathy, compassion, and using our talents to make the world a better place.

As Madison Steiner continues to expand her efforts and reach new heights with Peach's Neet Feet, her legacy of love, hope, and creativity will undoubtedly continue to inspire and uplift future generations.

Chapter 21: Om Prakash Sharma

Om Prakash Sharma is a name that might refer to several individuals across different fields in India, but if we focus on Om Prakash Sharma, the celebrated author of Hindi detective fiction, we uncover a fascinating figure in Indian literature. Sharma, popularly known for his thrilling and engaging stories, has been a significant influence on the genre of crime and detective fiction in Hindi literature. His works have not only entertained generations of readers but have also contributed to the development of popular literature in India. In this detailed exploration, we will delve into the life and career of Om Prakash Sharma, his literary contributions, the themes and styles of his work, and his impact on Indian literature.

Early Life and Background

Om Prakash Sharma was born in 1924 in the small town of Muzaffarnagar in Uttar Pradesh, India. His early life was marked by the rich cultural and literary traditions of northern India, which greatly influenced his future career as a writer. From a young age, Sharma displayed a keen interest in reading and storytelling, often immersing himself in the works of classical and contemporary Hindi literature.

Entry into the Literary World

Sharma's journey into the world of writing began in the 1950s when he started working as a journalist. His experiences as a journalist, where he encountered various facets of human life and society, provided him with a wealth of material and inspiration for his writing. However, it was his passion for detective stories and crime fiction that led him to carve a niche for himself in the literary world.

In the 1960s, Sharma began writing detective novels and quickly gained popularity for his gripping narratives, complex characters, and suspenseful plots. His books were well-received by readers, who were captivated by his ability to weave intricate mysteries that kept them on the edge of their seats.

Major Works and Characters

Om Prakash Sharma authored over 300 novels during his prolific career, making him one of the most productive and widely-read authors in Hindi detective fiction. Some of his most notable works include "Andhakar ka Beta," "Mujrim No. 100," and "Kala Admi." These novels, characterized by their fast-paced action, clever plot twists, and engaging prose, have become classics of the genre.

One of Sharma's most famous characters is "Rajesh," a suave and intelligent detective who appears in many of his novels. Rajesh, often compared to Western counterparts like Sherlock Holmes and Hercule Poirot, is known for his sharp intellect, keen observation skills, and unwavering commitment to justice. Through Rajesh, Sharma was able to explore various aspects of crime and criminal psychology, while also reflecting on broader social issues.

Themes and Style

Sharma's novels are known for their intricate plots and deep psychological insights. He had a knack for creating suspenseful atmospheres and keeping readers guessing until the very end. His writing style, marked by its clarity, simplicity, and engaging narrative, made his books accessible to a wide audience, including young readers.

Exploration of Social Issues

Beyond the thrilling mysteries, Sharma's novels often delve into various social issues and human psychology. He used the crime fiction genre as a lens to examine the darker aspects of society, such as corruption, greed, and moral decay. His stories frequently highlight the conflict between good and evil, the complexities of human nature, and the consequences of one's actions.

Influence on Hindi Literature

Om Prakash Sharma's contributions to Hindi literature extend beyond his detective novels. He played a crucial role in popularizing the genre of crime fiction in Hindi, inspiring a new generation of writers and readers. His success demonstrated that popular fiction could be both entertaining and thought-provoking, paving the way for other authors to explore similar themes.

Sharma's works also contributed to the development of Hindi prose, enriching the language with his vivid descriptions, compelling dialogues, and innovative storytelling techniques. His novels, which often incorporated elements of Indian culture and traditions, resonated with readers and helped to establish a distinct identity for Hindi detective fiction.

Legacy and Impact

Om Prakash Sharma passed away in 1998, but his legacy continues to live on through his extensive body of work. His novels remain popular among readers of all ages, and his influence can be seen in the works of contemporary Hindi crime fiction writers.

Recognition and Awards

Throughout his career, Sharma received numerous accolades for his contributions to literature. His works were widely acclaimed by both critics and readers, earning him a place among the most respected authors in Hindi literature. In recognition of his literary achievements, he was honored with several prestigious awards, including the Sahitya Akademi Award.

Continuing Relevance

In an era dominated by digital media and instant entertainment, Om Prakash Sharma's novels continue to captivate readers with their timeless appeal. The themes and issues he explored remain relevant today, reflecting the ongoing struggles between good and evil, justice and corruption, and human nature's complexities.

Conclusion

In conclusion, Om Prakash Sharma's life and career as a pioneering figure in Hindi detective fiction have left an indelible mark on Indian literature. Through his captivating novels, memorable characters, and exploration of social issues, he has enriched the literary landscape and inspired countless readers and writers. His legacy serves as a testament to the power of storytelling and the enduring appeal of crime fiction in Hindi literature.

Chapter 22: Sophie Cruz

Sophie Cruz is an inspiring young activist whose courage and advocacy have captured global attention. Born to undocumented immigrant parents from Oaxaca, Mexico, Sophie has become a symbol of hope and resilience in the fight for immigrant rights in the United States. Her journey from a five-year-old girl handing a letter to Pope Francis to a celebrated young advocate underscores the profound impact that even the youngest voices can have on important social issues. In this comprehensive exploration, we will delve into Sophie Cruz's early life, her rise to prominence, the significance of her activism, her impact on the immigrant rights movement, and her continuing legacy.

Early Life and Background

Sophie Cruz was born on December 17, 2010, in Los Angeles, California. Her parents, Raul Cruz and Zoyla Cruz, are undocumented immigrants from Oaxaca, Mexico. They moved to the United States in search of better opportunities and a safer environment for their family. Despite the challenges that come with being undocumented, Sophie's parents have always emphasized the importance of education, community, and standing up for what is right.

Growing up, Sophie was acutely aware of the precarious situation her family faced due to their immigration status. She knew that at any moment, her parents could be taken away from her due to deportation. This fear and uncertainty fueled her desire to advocate for the rights of undocumented immigrants and to ensure that families like hers could stay together.

The Defining Moment: Meeting Pope Francis

Sophie Cruz's rise to prominence began on September 23, 2015, when Pope Francis visited Washington, D.C. At the time, Sophie was just five years old, but she already possessed a remarkable sense of purpose. Determined to deliver a message to the Pope about the plight of undocumented families in the United States, Sophie attended the Papal parade with her family, hoping to catch his attention.

In a moment that captured the world's imagination, Sophie managed to break through the security barriers and approach Pope Francis. A security guard initially held her back, but the Pope, seeing her determination, called her forward. Sophie handed him a letter and a drawing, which depicted her plea for the Pope's support in protecting immigrant families. The letter read, in part:

"I want to tell you that my heart is very sad because I am afraid that one day ICE will take my parents away from me. I have a right to live with my parents. I have a right to be happy. All immigrants just like my dad help feed this country. They deserve to live with dignity. They deserve to live with respect."

This powerful act of courage and the poignant simplicity of her message resonated deeply with people around the world, highlighting the human side of the immigration debate.

Advocacy and Activism

Following her meeting with Pope Francis, Sophie Cruz continued to advocate for the rights of undocumented immigrants. Her story gained widespread media attention, making her a prominent voice in the immigrant rights movement. Despite her young age, Sophie demonstrated an extraordinary ability to articulate her experiences and the challenges faced by her family and other undocumented immigrants.

Sophie has participated in numerous rallies, marches, and public speaking events, where she has shared her story and called for comprehensive immigration reform. She has addressed large crowds and influential leaders, consistently emphasizing the need for policies that protect immigrant families and ensure their right to live without fear of deportation.

The DAPA Program and Supreme Court Involvement

One of the key issues that Sophie Cruz has advocated for is the Deferred Action for Parents of Americans and Lawful Permanent Residents (DAPA) program. Proposed by President Barack Obama in 2014, DAPA aimed to provide temporary relief from deportation and work authorization to certain undocumented parents of U.S. citizens and lawful permanent residents.

Sophie's advocacy included supporting the DAPA program and urging the Supreme Court to uphold it. In 2016, she and her family traveled to Washington, D.C., to participate in rallies and to raise awareness about the importance of the program. Unfortunately, the Supreme Court ended in a 4-4 deadlock, effectively blocking the implementation of DAPA.

Despite this setback, Sophie remained undeterred. Her unwavering commitment to the cause continued to inspire others and to bring attention to the need for comprehensive immigration reform.

Recognitions and Awards

Sophie's courage and dedication have not gone unnoticed. She has received numerous awards and recognitions for her activism. In 2017, she was honored with the Robert F. Kennedy Human Rights Award, which recognizes individuals who demonstrate significant contributions to human rights and social justice. This prestigious award highlighted Sophie's impact and the importance of her advocacy work.

In addition to formal recognitions, Sophie has been celebrated in various media outlets, including newspapers, television programs, and documentaries. Her story has been featured in The New York Times, The Washington Post, and Time magazine, among others. These platforms have helped amplify her message and have brought greater awareness to the issues faced by undocumented immigrants.

Public Speaking and Media Appearances

Sophie's ability to connect with audiences and convey powerful messages has made her a sought-after speaker. She has spoken at numerous events, including the Women's March, the United We

Dream Congress, and the Families Belong Together rally. Her speeches often emphasize the importance of family unity, the contributions of immigrants to society, and the need for compassionate immigration policies.

One of her most notable speeches was delivered at the Women's March on January 21, 2017, in Washington, D.C. Standing before a massive crowd, Sophie confidently declared:

"We are here together making a chain of love to protect our families. Let's keep together and fight for our rights. God is with us."

Her words resonated with the crowd and underscored the importance of solidarity and collective action in the face of adversity.

Educational Impact and Influence

Beyond her activism, Sophie Cruz's story has had a significant impact on education and youth empowerment. She has inspired countless young people to become involved in social justice issues and to use their voices to advocate for change. Her example demonstrates that age is not a barrier to making a difference and that even the youngest members of society can contribute to important conversations about justice and equality.

Educators and organizations have used Sophie's story as a teaching tool to discuss topics such as immigration, human rights, and civic engagement. Her experiences provide a relatable and powerful example of the impact that one individual can have on their community and the world.

Continuing Advocacy and Future Aspirations

As Sophie Cruz grows older, her commitment to advocacy shows no signs of waning. She continues to be an active participant in the immigrant rights movement, using her platform to raise awareness and to advocate for policy changes that protect and support immigrant families.

Looking to the future, Sophie has expressed a desire to continue her education and to pursue a career that allows her to help others. She has shown an interest in law and social work, fields that align with her passion for justice and her dedication to making a positive impact in her community.

The Broader Impact of Sophie Cruz's Advocacy

Sophie Cruz's advocacy has had a profound impact on the immigrant rights movement in several key ways:

1. **Humanizing the Immigration Debate**: By sharing her personal story, Sophie has put a human face on the immigration issue, highlighting the real-life consequences of immigration policies on families and children. Her experiences remind policymakers and the public that behind every statistic are individuals and families with hopes, dreams, and fears.

2. **Inspiring Youth Activism**: Sophie's courage and determination have inspired a new generation of young activists to become involved in social justice causes. Her story demonstrates that young people can be powerful advocates for change and that their voices are vital in the fight for justice and equality.

3. **Building Coalitions and Solidarity**: Sophie's participation in rallies, marches, and public speaking events has helped to build coalitions and solidarity among diverse groups fighting for immigrant rights. Her message of love, unity, and compassion resonates across different communities and has strengthened the movement for comprehensive immigration reform.

4. **Advocating for Policy Change**: Through her advocacy, Sophie has brought attention to specific policies and programs that impact undocumented immigrants, such as DAPA and DACA (Deferred Action for Childhood Arrivals). Her efforts have helped to mobilize support for

these programs and to push for broader legislative changes that protect immigrant families.

Conclusion

In conclusion, Sophie Cruz's journey from a five-year-old girl handing a letter to Pope Francis to a prominent young activist is a powerful testament to the impact of courage, compassion, and advocacy. Her story underscores the importance of standing up for what is right and the profound influence that even the youngest voices can have on important social issues.

Sophie's unwavering commitment to the fight for immigrant rights has brought hope and inspiration to countless individuals and families. Her advocacy has humanized the immigration debate, inspired youth activism, built coalitions, and pushed for policy changes that protect and support immigrant families.

As Sophie Cruz continues her journey, her legacy of love, unity, and justice will undoubtedly inspire future generations to advocate for a more compassionate and equitable world. Her story reminds us all that we have the power to make a difference and that even the smallest voices can create significant change.

Chapter 23: Xóchitl Guadalupe Cruz

Xóchitl Guadalupe Cruz López is a remarkable young inventor and environmental activist from San Cristóbal de las Casas, a city in the southern Mexican state of Chiapas. At just eight years old, Xóchitl gained international recognition for her innovative use of recycled materials to create solar-powered water heaters, devices that have significantly improved the quality of life for families in her community. Her ingenuity, passion for sustainability, and commitment to addressing environmental challenges have made her a symbol of hope and inspiration for young people around the world. In this comprehensive exploration, we will delve into Xóchitl Guadalupe Cruz's background, her groundbreaking inventions, the impact of her work on her community, and her ongoing efforts to promote environmental awareness and sustainable development.

Early Life and Inspiration

Xóchitl Guadalupe Cruz López was born on December 24, 2007, in San Cristóbal de las Casas, Chiapas, Mexico. From a young age, Xóchitl showed a keen interest in science and technology, inspired by her father, who worked as a bricklayer and introduced her to the principles of engineering and construction. Growing up in a region where access to basic amenities like electricity and clean water was limited, Xóchitl became acutely aware of the environmental challenges facing her community and the importance of finding sustainable solutions.

The Invention of Solar-Powered Water Heaters

In 2018, at the age of eight, Xóchitl Guadalupe Cruz gained international attention for her invention of solar-powered water heaters made from recycled materials. The idea for the project came to her when she noticed that many families in her community relied on wood-fired stoves to heat water, a process that not only consumed large amounts of wood but also contributed to deforestation and indoor air pollution.

Determined to find a sustainable alternative, Xóchitl began experimenting with different materials and designs. Drawing on her father's knowledge of construction, she created a prototype of a solar-powered water heater using discarded bottles, aluminum foil, and other recycled materials. The device worked by harnessing the sun's energy to heat water stored in the bottles, providing a clean and environmentally friendly source of hot water for households.

Impact on the Community

Xóchitl's solar-powered water heaters quickly gained popularity in her community, offering an affordable and eco-friendly solution to the problem of access to hot water. Families who had previously relied on wood-fired stoves or costly electric heaters were now able to enjoy the benefits of solar energy, saving money on fuel costs and reducing their carbon footprint.

The impact of Xóchitl's invention extended beyond just providing hot water; it also helped to raise awareness about the importance of environmental sustainability and the potential of renewable energy technologies. Her project inspired other young people in Chiapas and beyond to explore ways of using recycled materials and renewable energy sources to address environmental challenges in their own communities.

Recognition and Awards

Xóchitl Guadalupe Cruz's innovative work has earned her widespread recognition and numerous awards both nationally and internationally. In 2018, she was awarded the prestigious Environmental Youth Prize by the United Nations for her outstanding contribution to environmental conservation and sustainable development. The award not only celebrated Xóchitl's achievements but also highlighted the potential of young people to drive positive change in their communities.

In addition to the UN prize, Xóchitl has been honored with various other awards and accolades, including the National Children's Award for Environmental Conservation in Mexico. Her story has been featured in media outlets around the world, shining a spotlight on her ingenuity and inspiring other young inventors to follow in her footsteps.

Continuing Innovation and Advocacy

Despite her young age, Xóchitl Guadalupe Cruz remains committed to using her talents and creativity to address environmental challenges and promote sustainable development. She continues to explore new ideas and inventions, seeking ways to harness the power of renewable energy and recycled materials to improve the lives of people in her community and beyond.

In addition to her innovative projects, Xóchitl is also actively involved in advocacy and education efforts aimed at raising awareness about environmental issues and inspiring others to take action. She has participated in various conferences, workshops, and public speaking events, where she shares her experiences and encourages young people to become agents of change in their communities.

Legacy and Inspiration

Xóchitl Guadalupe Cruz's legacy extends far beyond her inventions; she has become a symbol of hope and inspiration for young people around the world. Her story demonstrates the power of ingenuity, determination, and compassion to effect positive change in the world, regardless of age or background.

Through her innovative projects and advocacy efforts, Xóchitl has shown that even the smallest actions can have a big impact on environmental conservation and sustainable development. Her example has inspired countless young people to explore their own passions and talents and to use them to make a difference in their communities.

Conclusion

In conclusion, Xóchitl Guadalupe Cruz López's journey from a curious eight-year-old girl to an internationally recognized inventor and environmental activist is a testament to the power of creativity, determination, and compassion. Her innovative use of recycled materials to create solar-powered water heaters has not only improved the quality of life for families in her community but has also inspired a global movement for environmental conservation and sustainable development.

As she continues her work, Xóchitl serves as a shining example of the potential of young people to drive positive change in the world. Her story reminds us that we all have a role to play in protecting the planet and building a more sustainable future for generations to come.

Chapter 24: Jessica Watson

Jessica Watson is an Australian sailor whose name became synonymous with courage, determination, and resilience when she became the youngest person to sail solo, non-stop, and unassisted around the world. Born on May 18, 1993, in Queensland, Australia, Jessica's extraordinary voyage captured the world's attention and inspired millions with her indomitable spirit and adventurous spirit. In this detailed exploration, we will delve into Jessica Watson's background, her historic solo circumnavigation, the challenges she faced along the way, the impact of her achievement, and her ongoing contributions to sailing and youth empowerment.

Early Life and Introduction to Sailing

Jessica Watson's love for the sea was evident from a young age. Growing up in Queensland, Australia, she was surrounded by water and developed a deep connection to the ocean. At just eight years old, Jessica began sailing with her family, quickly falling in love with the sport and the sense of freedom it provided.

As she honed her sailing skills, Jessica set her sights on bigger challenges, dreaming of one day sailing solo around the world. Despite her youth, she was determined to pursue her passion and prove that age was no barrier to achieving her goals.

The Solo Circumnavigation

Jessica Watson's historic solo circumnavigation began on October 18, 2009, when she set sail from Sydney, Australia, aboard her yacht, "Ella's Pink Lady." At the age of just 16, Jessica embarked on a journey that would take her across some of the world's most treacherous oceans and challenging conditions.

Over the course of 210 days, Jessica navigated her way through storms, rough seas, and solitude, facing countless obstacles along the way. Despite the physical and mental challenges, she remained focused and determined, drawing strength from her love of sailing and her unwavering belief in herself.

Challenges and Triumphs

Jessica Watson's solo circumnavigation was not without its challenges. From battling fierce storms in the Southern Ocean to navigating busy shipping lanes and contending with sleep deprivation, she encountered numerous obstacles that tested her resilience and determination.

One of the most harrowing moments of Jessica's voyage came when her yacht was struck by a 63,000-ton cargo ship off the coast of Queensland. Despite sustaining damage to her vessel, Jessica managed to repair it and continue her journey, demonstrating remarkable resourcefulness and composure in the face of adversity.

Throughout her voyage, Jessica experienced moments of triumph and moments of doubt. There were times when she questioned her decision to undertake such a daunting challenge, but she never wavered in her determination to see it through to the end.

The Homecoming

On May 15, 2010, Jessica Watson made history when she sailed back into Sydney Harbor, completing her solo circumnavigation and becoming the youngest person to achieve such a feat. Her arrival was met with jubilant celebrations and widespread acclaim, as people around the world marveled at her courage and tenacity.

Jessica's triumphant return marked the culmination of years of preparation, sacrifice, and hard work. Her achievement not only shattered stereotypes and defied expectations but also inspired a new generation of young sailors to pursue their dreams and push the boundaries of what is possible.

Impact and Legacy

Jessica Watson's solo circumnavigation captured the imagination of people around the world and left a lasting impact on the sailing community and beyond. Her remarkable journey inspired millions with its message of courage, determination, and perseverance in the face of adversity.

Beyond the world of sailing, Jessica's achievement served as a powerful reminder of the potential of young people to achieve extraordinary things. Her story resonated with people of all ages and backgrounds, inspiring them to pursue their passions, overcome obstacles, and embrace the spirit of adventure.

Post-Circumnavigation

Following her historic solo circumnavigation, Jessica Watson continued to pursue her passion for sailing and adventure. She went on to compete in various sailing races and regattas, further cementing her status as one of Australia's most accomplished sailors.

In addition to her sailing endeavors, Jessica has become a sought-after motivational speaker, sharing her experiences and insights with audiences around the world. She has also written several books, including her memoir, "True Spirit," which chronicles her epic journey and the lessons she learned along the way.

Contributions to Youth Empowerment

In recent years, Jessica Watson has focused on empowering young people to pursue their dreams and embrace life's challenges with confidence and resilience. Through her speaking engagements, mentorship programs, and advocacy work, she encourages young people to step outside their comfort zones, take risks, and believe in themselves.

Jessica's own journey serves as a powerful example of the transformative power of determination and perseverance. By sharing her story and insights, she hopes to inspire the next generation of adventurers, explorers, and leaders to follow their passions and make their mark on the world.

Conclusion

In conclusion, Jessica Watson's historic solo circumnavigation stands as a testament to the power of courage, determination, and resilience. Her remarkable journey captured the world's imagination and inspired millions with its message of hope, adventure, and possibility.

Through her epic voyage, Jessica shattered stereotypes, defied expectations, and showed the world what is possible when you dare to dream big and believe in yourself. Her achievement not only made her a sailing legend but also left a lasting legacy of inspiration and empowerment for generations to come.

Chapter 25: Aung San Suu Kyi

Aung San Suu Kyi is a prominent political leader and Nobel Peace Prize laureate from Myanmar (formerly Burma), known for her steadfast commitment to democracy and human rights. Born into a politically significant family, she rose to international prominence as a symbol of peaceful resistance in the face of oppression. However, her legacy has become more complex and controversial in recent years due to her handling of the Rohingya crisis. This detailed exploration will delve into her early life, political career, activism, the international recognition she received, the challenges and controversies she faced, and her ongoing influence on Myanmar and the world.

Early Life and Background

Aung San Suu Kyi was born on June 19, 1945, in Rangoon (now Yangon), Myanmar. She is the daughter of Aung San, a revered Burmese independence hero who played a crucial role in negotiating Burma's independence from British colonial rule. Tragically, Aung San was assassinated in 1947, when Suu Kyi was just two years old. Her mother, Khin Kyi, was a prominent figure in her own right, later serving as Burma's ambassador to India and Nepal.

Growing up in a politically active household, Suu Kyi was immersed in discussions about her country's future from a young age. She pursued higher education in India, attending Lady Shri Ram College in New Delhi, and later studied philosophy, politics, and economics at St Hugh's College, Oxford. In 1972, she married Michael Aris, a British scholar, and the couple had two sons, Alexander and Kim.

Political Awakening and Activism

Aung San Suu Kyi's return to Burma in 1988 marked a turning point in her life and the country's political landscape. She came back to care for her ailing mother, but her arrival coincided with a massive pro-democracy uprising against the military dictatorship that had ruled Burma since 1962. Inspired by the widespread call for democratic reforms and propelled by her father's legacy, Suu Kyi quickly emerged as a leading figure in the movement.

In September 1988, she co-founded the National League for Democracy (NLD), aiming to establish a democratic government through peaceful means. Her eloquent speeches, advocating for non-violent resistance and democratic principles, galvanized millions of Burmese citizens. Her approach was heavily influenced by Mahatma Gandhi's philosophy of non-violence and civil disobedience.

House Arrest and International Recognition

The military junta, fearing her growing influence, placed Suu Kyi under house arrest in July 1989. This marked the beginning of a long period of detention, with intermittent releases and re-arrests spanning nearly two decades. Despite her confinement, she continued to inspire the pro-democracy movement, and her plight drew international attention.

In 1991, Suu Kyi was awarded the Nobel Peace Prize, which significantly amplified global awareness of her struggle. The Nobel Committee praised her "non-violent struggle for democracy and human rights," and she became an international symbol of peaceful resistance against tyranny. The prize money was used to establish a health and education trust for the Burmese people.

Political Landscape and Partial Freedom

During her years of house arrest, the NLD remained active, although it faced severe repression. The party won a landslide victory in the 1990 general elections, securing 81% of the seats in parliament. However, the military refused to recognize the results and maintained its grip on power.

In November 2010, after intense international pressure and domestic advocacy, Aung San Suu Kyi was finally released from house arrest. Her release was met with widespread jubilation in Myanmar and welcomed by the international community. She soon resumed her role as the leader of the NLD and continued to push for democratic reforms.

2012 By-Elections and Parliamentary Role

A significant milestone came in April 2012 when the NLD participated in parliamentary by-elections. The party won 43 out of 45 available seats, and Aung San Suu Kyi herself was elected to the Pyithu Hluttaw, the lower house of Myanmar's parliament. This victory marked a turning point in the country's political landscape, signaling a shift towards democratic governance.

Her presence in parliament allowed her to work within the system to advocate for legal and constitutional reforms. However, her influence was still limited by the military's continued dominance, as the 2008 constitution reserved 25% of parliamentary seats for the military and gave it control over key ministries.

2015 General Elections and Leadership

The 2015 general elections were a landmark moment in Myanmar's history. The NLD secured a decisive victory, winning a majority of the seats in both houses of parliament. Although the constitution barred Aung San Suu Kyi from becoming president due to her marriage to a foreign national, she assumed the role of State Counsellor, a position created specifically for her that allowed her to act as the de facto leader of the country.

Under her leadership, Myanmar saw a period of cautious optimism. Efforts were made to implement economic reforms, improve healthcare and education, and encourage foreign investment. However, the military retained significant power, particularly in areas of national security and internal affairs.

The Rohingya Crisis and International Criticism

Aung San Suu Kyi's international reputation suffered a severe blow due to her handling of the Rohingya crisis. The Rohingya, a Muslim minority group in Myanmar's Rakhine State, faced brutal military crackdowns in 2016 and 2017, which the United Nations described as a "textbook example of ethnic cleansing." The violence led to the displacement of over 700,000 Rohingya, who fled to neighboring Bangladesh amid reports of mass killings, rapes, and the burning of villages.

Despite international outcry, Suu Kyi largely defended the military's actions, framing the crisis as a counter-terrorism effort and downplaying allegations of human rights abuses. Her failure to unequivocally condemn the violence and address the plight of the Rohingya drew sharp criticism from human rights organizations, foreign governments, and global figures. Many argued that her silence and complicity contradicted the principles of human rights and democracy she once championed.

Legal Proceedings and Ongoing Challenges

In 2019, The Gambia brought a case against Myanmar at the International Court of Justice (ICJ), accusing it of violating the Genocide Convention in its treatment of the Rohingya. Aung San Suu Kyi traveled to The Hague to defend her country, arguing that the allegations were based on incomplete information and that Myanmar's actions were directed at combating insurgency, not targeting civilians. The ICJ, however, ordered Myanmar to take provisional measures to protect the Rohingya from further harm.

The Rohingya crisis remains a dark chapter in Aung San Suu Kyi's legacy. It highlighted the complexities and limitations of her leadership in a country where the military continues to wield significant power.

Military Coup and Detention

On February 1, 2021, Myanmar's military staged a coup d'état, detaining Aung San Suu Kyi and other senior NLD leaders. The military justified the coup by alleging widespread voter fraud in the November 2020 general elections, which the NLD had won decisively. Independent observers, however, found no evidence to support these claims.

The coup sparked nationwide protests and a brutal military crackdown, leading to widespread violence, arrests, and the deaths of hundreds of civilians. Suu Kyi was charged with various offenses, including violating COVID-19 regulations and illegally importing walkie-talkies, charges widely viewed as politically motivated.

Legacy and Influence

Aung San Suu Kyi's legacy is multifaceted and complex. Her early years of peaceful resistance and unwavering commitment to democratic principles earned her global admiration and the Nobel Peace Prize. She became a beacon of hope for those fighting against oppression and a symbol of the power of non-violent protest.

However, her later years in power, particularly her handling of the Rohingya crisis, tarnished her international reputation and led to significant criticism. The contrast between her image as a human rights icon and her actions (or inactions) as a political leader highlighted the complexities and challenges of governing a deeply divided and militarized country.

Continuing Influence

Despite the controversies, Aung San Suu Kyi remains an influential figure in Myanmar. Her imprisonment and the military coup have galvanized many of her supporters, leading to ongoing resistance against military rule. Her plight continues to draw international attention, underscoring the ongoing struggle for democracy in Myanmar.

Her story serves as a powerful reminder of the challenges and contradictions that often accompany political leadership, especially in countries with deep-seated conflicts and authoritarian legacies. It also highlights the enduring importance of human rights and the need for continued vigilance and advocacy in the face of oppression.

Conclusion

Aung San Suu Kyi's journey from a political prisoner to the de facto leader of Myanmar is a testament to her resilience, courage, and dedication to her country's democratic aspirations. Her life and career embody both the triumphs and the complexities of the fight for human rights and democracy. While her legacy is marred by the Rohingya crisis, her contributions to the struggle for democracy in Myanmar cannot be overlooked.

Her story is one of profound human courage and frailty, illustrating the extraordinary possibilities and profound challenges of leadership. It serves as an important case study for understanding the dynamics of political power, the role of international diplomacy, and the ongoing quest for justice and human rights in the modern world.

Chapter 26: Hannah Taylor

Hannah Taylor is a Canadian activist and social entrepreneur who gained international recognition for her work in addressing homelessness and advocating for the rights of those experiencing homelessness. Born in Winnipeg, Manitoba, in 1996, Hannah's journey began at a young age when she was deeply moved by the sight of a homeless man on the streets of her city. This encounter sparked a lifelong commitment to making a difference in the lives of those less fortunate and led her to found the Ladybug Foundation at the age of just eight. In this detailed exploration, we will delve into Hannah Taylor's background, her founding of the Ladybug Foundation, her advocacy efforts, the impact of her work, and her ongoing contributions to addressing homelessness and poverty.

Early Life and Inspiration

Hannah Taylor's passion for helping others was ignited at the tender age of five when she encountered a homeless man on the streets of Winnipeg. Struck by his plight and moved by compassion, she asked her mother why someone would be living on the streets and what she could do to help. This encounter planted the seed for what would later become her life's mission.

Founding of the Ladybug Foundation

At just eight years old, Hannah Taylor founded the Ladybug Foundation, a charitable organization dedicated to raising awareness about homelessness and supporting initiatives to alleviate poverty. The name "Ladybug" was inspired by Hannah's belief that every person deserves to have a safe place to call home, just like the ladybug's shell provides shelter and protection.

With the help of her family and community supporters, Hannah embarked on a journey to raise awareness about homelessness and inspire action to address its root causes. She began by selling homemade ladybug pins to raise funds for shelters and food programs, leveraging her youthful enthusiasm and infectious passion to make a difference.

Advocacy Efforts

As Hannah Taylor's profile grew, so too did her advocacy efforts. She became a sought-after speaker at schools, community events, and conferences, where she shared her personal story and spoke passionately about the need to end homelessness. Her eloquence and sincerity resonated with audiences of all ages, inspiring countless individuals to get involved in the fight against poverty and homelessness.

In addition to her speaking engagements, Hannah launched various awareness campaigns and initiatives through the Ladybug Foundation. These included fundraising events, educational programs, and outreach efforts aimed at challenging stereotypes and misconceptions about homelessness and promoting empathy and compassion for those in need.

Impact of Her Work

Hannah Taylor's work through the Ladybug Foundation has had a significant impact on communities across Canada and beyond. Through her advocacy and fundraising efforts, she has raised millions of dollars for homeless shelters, food programs, and support services, helping to provide vital resources to individuals and families in need.

More importantly, Hannah's work has helped to raise awareness about the root causes of homelessness and the importance of addressing issues such as poverty, affordable housing, and mental health. By challenging stigma and promoting understanding, she has contributed to a more compassionate and inclusive society that recognizes the inherent dignity and worth of every individual.

Recognition and Awards

Hannah Taylor's tireless dedication and commitment to social change have earned her numerous awards and accolades. In 2007, she was named one of "Canada's Top 20 Under 20" by Youth in Motion, recognizing her as one of the country's most inspiring young leaders. She has also received the Princess Diana Legacy Award and the Governor General's Caring Canadian Award, among others.

In addition to formal recognition, Hannah's story has been featured in media outlets around the world, bringing greater attention to the issue of homelessness and amplifying her message of compassion and empathy. Her impact extends far beyond her hometown of Winnipeg, inspiring individuals and communities to take action and make a difference in the lives of others.

Continuing Contributions

Despite her young age, Hannah Taylor remains deeply committed to her advocacy work and continues to make significant contributions to addressing homelessness and poverty. In addition to her ongoing involvement with the Ladybug Foundation, she has expanded her efforts to include initiatives focused on education, empowerment, and systemic change.

Hannah is actively involved in advocacy campaigns and policy discussions aimed at addressing the root causes of homelessness and advocating for social justice and equality. She works closely with government officials, community leaders, and grassroots organizations to develop solutions that promote housing affordability, economic opportunity, and access to essential services.

Legacy and Inspiration

Hannah Taylor's legacy extends far beyond her achievements as a social entrepreneur and activist. She has inspired a generation of young people to become engaged in social issues, speak out against injustice, and work towards positive change in their communities. Her story serves as a powerful reminder of the impact that one person, regardless of age, can have on the world.

Through her unwavering determination, compassion, and advocacy, Hannah has helped to change the conversation around homelessness and poverty, challenging stereotypes and inspiring empathy and action. Her work continues to shine a light on the need for greater social and economic justice and serves as a beacon of hope for those working to build a more just and equitable society.

Conclusion

In conclusion, Hannah Taylor's journey from a compassionate young girl to a leading advocate for homelessness and poverty is a testament to the power of empathy, passion, and determination. Through her work with the Ladybug Foundation, she has made a significant impact on communities across Canada and beyond, raising awareness, inspiring action, and challenging stereotypes.

Her legacy as a social entrepreneur and activist will continue to inspire future generations to stand up for what they believe in, speak out against injustice, and work towards a more compassionate and inclusive world. Hannah Taylor's story is a reminder that no matter how young or inexperienced we may be, we all have the power to make a difference in the lives of others and create positive change in the world.

Chapter 27: Ryan Hickman

Ryan Hickman is an extraordinary young environmentalist who gained worldwide recognition for his passionate advocacy for recycling and environmental conservation. Born on May 16, 2007, in Orange County, California, Ryan's journey towards becoming a prominent eco-activist began at the tender age of three when he accompanied his father on a trip to a local recycling center. This experience sparked his fascination with recycling, leading him to embark on a mission to clean up the environment and protect wildlife by collecting and recycling plastic bottles and other waste materials. In this detailed exploration, we will delve into Ryan Hickman's background, his journey towards becoming a recycling advocate, his impact on environmental conservation, and his ongoing efforts to inspire others to join the fight against plastic pollution.

Early Life and Inspiration

Ryan Hickman's passion for recycling was ignited during a visit to a recycling center with his father, Damion Hickman, at the age of three. Fascinated by the process of turning recyclables into new products, Ryan became determined to make a difference in the world by collecting and recycling as much waste as possible.

With the support of his parents, Ryan started his own recycling business, Ryan's Recycling Company, at the age of four. Armed with a small wagon and an infectious enthusiasm for environmental conservation, he began collecting recyclables from friends, family, and neighbors in his local community.

Ryan's Recycling Company

Ryan's Recycling Company quickly gained momentum as word spread about the young entrepreneur's mission to clean up the environment. What began as a small-scale operation in the Hickman family's garage soon grew into a full-fledged recycling business, complete with a dedicated sorting area and storage space for recyclables.

With the help of his parents and volunteers, Ryan expanded his recycling efforts to local businesses, schools, and community events, collecting thousands of pounds of recyclables each week. He sorted and processed the materials himself, meticulously separating plastics, glass, and aluminum to ensure they were properly recycled.

Environmental Advocacy

As Ryan's Recycling Company continued to grow, so too did Ryan's passion for environmental advocacy. He became a vocal spokesperson for recycling and environmental conservation, sharing his message with audiences of all ages through speaking engagements, interviews, and social media.

Ryan's infectious enthusiasm and genuine commitment to making a difference inspired people around the world to join the fight against plastic pollution. He emphasized the importance of reducing, reusing, and recycling waste to protect the planet for future generations and encouraged others to take action in their own communities.

Impact on Environmental Conservation

Ryan Hickman's impact on environmental conservation has been nothing short of remarkable. Through his tireless efforts, he has diverted thousands of pounds of recyclable materials from landfills, reducing waste and preventing pollution in his local community and beyond.

In addition to his direct impact on waste reduction, Ryan's Recycling Company has helped to raise awareness about the importance of recycling and environmental stewardship. His story has been featured in numerous media outlets, shining a spotlight on the issue of plastic pollution and inspiring others to take action.

Recognition and Awards

Ryan Hickman's dedication to recycling and environmental advocacy has earned him widespread recognition and numerous awards and accolades. In 2017, he was named "Kid of the Year" by CNN Heroes, honoring his remarkable achievements and contributions to environmental conservation.

He has also received awards from organizations such as the National Waste and Recycling Association and the California State Assembly, recognizing his outstanding efforts to promote recycling and sustainability. Despite his young age, Ryan's impact on the environment has been recognized and celebrated by people around the world.

Ongoing Efforts

Despite his many accomplishments, Ryan Hickman remains committed to his mission of cleaning up the environment and protecting wildlife. He continues to run Ryan's Recycling Company, collecting and recycling recyclables from his community and promoting environmental awareness through speaking engagements and advocacy work.

In addition to his recycling efforts, Ryan has expanded his environmental advocacy to include initiatives aimed at reducing single-use plastics and promoting sustainable living practices. He is actively involved in campaigns to ban plastic straws and bags, raise awareness about the importance of ocean conservation, and empower young people to become environmental stewards in their own communities.

Legacy and Inspiration

Ryan Hickman's legacy as an environmentalist and recycling advocate serves as an inspiration to people of all ages. His story demonstrates the power of one individual to make a positive impact on the world and highlights the importance of taking action to protect the environment for future generations.

Through his passion, determination, and unwavering commitment to environmental conservation, Ryan has inspired millions of people to rethink their relationship with waste and take steps to reduce their environmental footprint. His message of hope and optimism resonates with people around the world, reminding us that we all have a role to play in building a more sustainable and resilient planet.

Conclusion

In conclusion, Ryan Hickman's journey from a curious young boy to a leading advocate for recycling and environmental conservation is a testament to the power of passion, determination, and perseverance. Through his remarkable achievements with Ryan's Recycling Company, he has demonstrated the profound impact that one person can have on the world and inspired others to join the fight against plastic pollution.

Ryan's story serves as a powerful reminder of the importance of environmental stewardship and the need to take action to protect the planet for future generations. His legacy will continue to inspire and empower people of all ages to make a difference in their communities and work towards a more sustainable and environmentally conscious world.

Chapter 28: Elif Bilgin

Elif Bilgin is a young Turkish scientist and inventor known for her innovative work in the field of bioplastics. Born on January 15, 1999, in Istanbul, Turkey, Elif gained international recognition at a young age for her groundbreaking research on creating biodegradable plastic from banana peels. Her work has earned her numerous awards and accolades, highlighting her as a rising star in the field of sustainable technology. In this detailed exploration, we will delve into Elif Bilgin's background, her innovative research on bioplastics, the impact of her work on environmental sustainability, and her ongoing contributions to science and innovation.

Early Life and Inspiration

Elif Bilgin's fascination with science and innovation began at a young age. Growing up in Istanbul, she was exposed to a wide range of scientific concepts and experiments through school and extracurricular activities. Inspired by her curiosity and a desire to make a positive impact on the world, Elif began exploring ways to use science and technology to address environmental challenges.

Bioplastic Research

Elif Bilgin's journey into the world of bioplastics began in high school when she became interested in finding alternative solutions to traditional plastics, which are known for their harmful environmental impact. Drawing inspiration from her surroundings, Elif focused her research on developing a biodegradable plastic using readily available and renewable resources.

After conducting extensive research and experimentation, Elif discovered that banana peels contain high levels of starch, which can be extracted and processed into a bioplastic material. She developed a novel method for extracting starch from banana peels and converting it into a biodegradable plastic that is both environmentally friendly and cost-effective.

Scientific Method and Innovation

Elif Bilgin's research exemplifies the scientific method in action, demonstrating the process of observation, hypothesis formation, experimentation, and analysis. Her innovative approach to bioplastic production involved a series of carefully designed experiments and iterations, as she refined her methods and optimized her results.

Through trial and error, Elif overcame numerous challenges and obstacles, including finding the most efficient method for extracting starch from banana peels and developing a process for turning the starch into a usable bioplastic material. Her dedication to scientific inquiry and her willingness to experiment and innovate were key factors in the success of her research.

Recognition and Awards

Elif Bilgin's groundbreaking research on bioplastics has earned her widespread recognition and numerous awards and accolades. In 2013, she was awarded the prestigious Science in Action award at the Google Science Fair, which recognizes young scientists who demonstrate exceptional creativity, innovation, and scientific inquiry.

Her work has also been recognized by organizations such as the European Commission, the United Nations, and the International Youth Science Forum, among others. In addition to receiving awards, Elif has been invited to speak at conferences and events around the world, where she shares her insights and experiences with aspiring young scientists and innovators.

Impact on Environmental Sustainability

Elif Bilgin's research on bioplastics has the potential to have a significant impact on environmental sustainability by providing a viable alternative to traditional plastics. Unlike conventional plastics, which are derived from fossil fuels and can take hundreds of years to decompose, bioplastics are made from renewable resources and are biodegradable, meaning they can break down naturally over time.

By developing a biodegradable plastic from banana peels, Elif has demonstrated the feasibility of using organic waste materials to create sustainable alternatives to traditional plastics. Her research has the potential to reduce the environmental impact of plastic pollution and contribute to the transition towards a more circular and sustainable economy.

Ongoing Contributions to Science and Innovation

Since her groundbreaking research on bioplastics, Elif Bilgin has continued to pursue her passion for science and innovation. She has expanded her research interests to include other areas of environmental sustainability, such as renewable energy, climate change mitigation, and biodiversity conservation.

In addition to her scientific work, Elif is actively involved in promoting STEM education and inspiring the next generation of scientists and innovators. She serves as a role model and mentor for young people around the world, encouraging them to pursue their interests in science, technology, engineering, and mathematics and make a positive impact on the world.

Conclusion

In conclusion, Elif Bilgin's journey from a curious high school student to a pioneering scientist and inventor is a testament to the power of passion, curiosity, and determination. Her groundbreaking research on bioplastics has the potential to revolutionize the way we think about plastic production and consumption and has earned her widespread recognition and acclaim.

Through her innovative approach to scientific inquiry and her commitment to environmental sustainability, Elif has demonstrated the transformative potential of science and technology in addressing global challenges. Her work serves as an inspiration to young people everywhere, showing them that they have the power to make a difference in the world through creativity, ingenuity, and perseverance.

As Elif continues to pursue her scientific research and advocacy efforts, her impact on environmental sustainability and innovation is sure to grow, leaving a lasting legacy for generations to come.

Chapter 29: Luis Soriano

Luis Soriano is a Colombian educator and activist renowned for his innovative approach to promoting literacy and education in remote and marginalized communities. Born in La Gloria, a rural village in Colombia's Caribbean region, Soriano grew up with a deep appreciation for the transformative power of education. Inspired by his own experiences and a desire to empower others through learning, he embarked on a mission to bring books to the children living in Colombia's rural areas, where access to education and resources is often limited. In this comprehensive exploration, we will delve into Luis Soriano's background, the creation of his Biblioburro (Donkey Library), his impact on education and literacy, the challenges he faced, and the enduring legacy of his work.

Early Life and Inspiration

Luis Soriano was born in La Gloria, a small village in the department of Bolivar, Colombia, in the 1970s. Growing up in a rural community with limited access to educational resources, Soriano understood the challenges faced by children in remote areas who aspired to learn and pursue an education. Despite the obstacles he encountered, Soriano was determined to overcome adversity and pursue his own education, recognizing its potential to open doors and create opportunities for a better future.

Creation of the Biblioburro

The idea for the Biblioburro, or Donkey Library, was born out of Soriano's passion for reading and his desire to share that passion with others. In 1990, Soriano, then a primary school teacher, began loading his donkeys, Alfa and Beto, with books from his personal collection and traveling to remote villages and settlements in the mountains of northern Colombia. Armed with a vision of bringing the world of books and knowledge to children who lacked access to libraries and schools, Soriano embarked on what would become his life's work.

The Biblioburro quickly gained popularity and recognition as it made its rounds through the countryside, stopping at schools, community centers, and even private homes to deliver books and educational materials to eager readers. Soriano's initiative captured the hearts and imaginations of people around the world, who were inspired by his dedication to spreading literacy and fostering a love of reading in underserved communities.

Impact on Education and Literacy

The impact of Luis Soriano's Biblioburro on education and literacy in rural Colombia cannot be overstated. Through his mobile library, Soriano has brought books, educational resources, and opportunities for learning to thousands of children and adults in remote areas who would otherwise have limited access to such materials. By instilling a love of reading and learning in the communities he serves, Soriano has empowered individuals to pursue their dreams, expand their horizons, and envision a brighter future for themselves and their families.

The Biblioburro has also had a profound effect on the communities it visits, fostering a sense of community and belonging among residents and strengthening social bonds through shared experiences of learning and discovery. Soriano's initiative has not only enriched the lives of individuals but has also contributed to the cultural and social fabric of rural Colombia, highlighting the transformative power of education and literacy in fostering positive social change.

Challenges and Adversities

Despite the widespread acclaim and admiration for his work, Luis Soriano has faced numerous challenges and adversities in his efforts to promote education and literacy in rural Colombia. From logistical hurdles such as navigating rugged terrain and inclement weather to financial constraints and bureaucratic obstacles, Soriano has encountered numerous obstacles along the way. However, his unwavering commitment to his mission and the support of his community have enabled him to overcome these challenges and continue his work against all odds.

In addition to logistical and financial challenges, Soriano has also faced skepticism and criticism from some quarters, with detractors questioning the efficacy and sustainability of his mobile library initiative. However, Soriano remains undeterred by criticism, focusing instead on the positive impact his work has had on the lives of countless individuals and communities.

Recognition and Awards

Luis Soriano's dedication to promoting education and literacy in rural Colombia has earned him widespread recognition and numerous awards and accolades. In 2007, he was honored with the Waislitz Global Citizen Award, which recognizes individuals who are making a positive impact on their communities and the world. He has also been featured in documentaries, books, and media outlets around the world, bringing attention to his inspiring story and the importance of his work.

In addition to formal recognition, Soriano's Biblioburro has been celebrated by people from all walks of life, who have been inspired by his selflessness, determination, and compassion. His story serves as a powerful reminder of the transformative power of education and the profound impact that one individual can have on the lives of others.

Legacy and Enduring Impact

Luis Soriano's legacy as a champion of education and literacy in rural Colombia is far-reaching and enduring. Through his pioneering efforts with the Biblioburro, Soriano has inspired countless individuals and organizations to take action to promote education and literacy in underserved communities around the world. His story serves as a powerful example of the difference that one person can make when they are driven by passion, compassion, and a commitment to social justice.

The Biblioburro continues to operate to this day, with Soriano and his donkeys making regular visits to communities in rural Colombia to deliver books and educational materials to eager readers. His work has inspired similar initiatives in other countries, where individuals and organizations are following in Soriano's footsteps to bring the joy of reading and learning to those who need it most.

Conclusion

In conclusion, Luis Soriano's Biblioburro is a shining example of the transformative power of education and the profound impact that one individual can have on their community and the world. Through his tireless efforts to promote literacy and learning in rural Colombia, Soriano has touched the lives of thousands of individuals and communities, empowering them to pursue their dreams and build a better future for themselves and their families.

Soriano's story serves as a powerful reminder of the importance of access to education and the role that libraries and literacy initiatives play in promoting social justice, equality, and opportunity. His legacy will continue to inspire future generations to take action to address the educational inequalities that persist in communities around the world, ensuring that all individuals have the opportunity to reach their full potential and contribute to the betterment of society.

Chapter 30: Sajid Hussein

Sajid Hussain Baloch was a Pakistani journalist and human rights activist known for his work on highlighting the issues faced by the Baloch people, particularly in the conflict-ridden region of Balochistan. Born and raised in Balochistan, Sajid Hussain dedicated his career to shedding light on the socio-political challenges and human rights abuses in the region, despite facing significant risks and threats to his personal safety. Tragically, Sajid Hussain disappeared in mysterious circumstances in March 2020 and was later found dead in Sweden, where he had been living in exile. His death sparked widespread outrage and raised concerns about the safety of journalists and activists who risk their lives to report on sensitive issues in Pakistan.

Early Life and Career

Sajid Hussain Baloch was born and raised in Balochistan, a province in southwestern Pakistan known for its natural resources and ongoing conflict between separatist groups, insurgents, and the Pakistani government. Growing up in this volatile region, Sajid developed a deep understanding of the socio-political dynamics and the challenges faced by the Baloch people, including poverty, marginalization, and human rights abuses.

Driven by a passion for journalism and a desire to amplify the voices of the marginalized, Sajid Hussain began his career as a journalist, focusing on issues related to human rights, social justice, and political activism. He worked for various media outlets in Pakistan, including newspapers and online platforms, where he reported on issues such as enforced disappearances, extrajudicial killings, and the struggle for autonomy in Balochistan.

Advocacy and Exile

As Sajid Hussain's reputation as a journalist and activist grew, so too did the threats to his safety. He faced harassment, intimidation, and violence from both state and non-state actors who sought to silence his reporting and activism. In response to the escalating risks, Sajid made the difficult decision to leave Pakistan and seek asylum abroad, fearing for his life and the safety of his family.

Sajid Hussain eventually settled in Sweden, where he continued his work as a journalist and advocate for the Baloch cause. Despite living in exile, he remained deeply committed to his mission of raising awareness about the human rights situation in Balochistan and advocating for justice and accountability for the victims of violence and oppression in the region.

Disappearance and Death

In March 2020, Sajid Hussain Baloch disappeared under mysterious circumstances while living in Uppsala, Sweden. His sudden disappearance sparked concern among his friends, colleagues, and supporters, who feared that he had been targeted for his activism and reporting on sensitive issues. Despite extensive search efforts and appeals for information, Sajid remained missing for weeks.

Tragically, in April 2020, Sajid Hussain's body was found in the Fyris River near Uppsala, Sweden. The circumstances of his death raised questions and suspicions about foul play, with many speculating that he had been targeted and murdered for his work as a journalist and activist. However, the exact cause and circumstances of his death remain unclear, and investigations into the case are ongoing.

Legacy and Impact

Sajid Hussain Baloch's untimely death sent shockwaves through the journalism and human rights communities in Pakistan and beyond. His courageous reporting and advocacy for the Baloch cause earned him admiration and respect from colleagues, activists, and supporters around the world. His death served as a stark reminder of the dangers faced by journalists and activists who dare to speak truth to power and expose human rights abuses and corruption.

In the wake of Sajid Hussain's death, calls for justice and accountability echoed across Pakistan and beyond, with demands for a thorough investigation into the circumstances surrounding his disappearance and death. His legacy continues to inspire journalists, activists, and advocates to carry on his work and fight for justice, transparency, and human rights in Balochistan and beyond.

Conclusion

Sajid Hussain Baloch's life and work as a journalist and human rights activist exemplify the courage, resilience, and commitment of individuals who dedicate themselves to shining a light on injustice and oppression. Despite facing grave risks and threats to his safety, Sajid remained steadfast in his pursuit of truth and justice for the Baloch people, leaving behind a legacy of courage, integrity, and unwavering commitment to human rights.

As investigations into his death continue and calls for justice grow louder, Sajid Hussain's memory serves as a poignant reminder of the sacrifices made by journalists and activists around the world in the pursuit of truth and justice. His legacy will endure as a beacon of hope and inspiration for future generations who carry on the struggle for human rights and social justice in Balochistan and beyond.

Chapter 31: Marley Dias

Marley Dias is a remarkable young activist, author, and entrepreneur known for her advocacy work promoting diversity in children's literature. Born on January 3, 2005, in Philadelphia, Pennsylvania, Marley gained international recognition at the age of 11 for her #1000BlackGirlBooks campaign, which aimed to collect and donate 1,000 books featuring black girls as the main characters. Since then, Marley has continued to be a powerful voice for change, using her platform to advocate for inclusivity, representation, and social justice. In this detailed exploration, we will delve into Marley Dias's background, the inspiration behind her activism, the impact of her #1000BlackGirlBooks campaign, her ongoing advocacy work, and her contributions to promoting diversity and representation in children's literature.

Early Life and Inspiration

Marley Dias was born and raised in West Orange, New Jersey, to parents Janice Johnson Dias and Scott Dias. From a young age, Marley developed a love for reading and storytelling, immersing herself in books and literature that sparked her imagination and curiosity. However, as a black girl growing up in the United States, Marley often found herself frustrated by the lack of diversity and representation in the books she read, which rarely featured characters who looked like her or shared her experiences.

Inspired by her own experiences and a desire to see more diverse and inclusive representations in children's literature, Marley embarked on a mission to collect and donate books featuring black girls as the main characters. Drawing on her passion for reading and her belief in the power of storytelling to inspire empathy and understanding, Marley launched the #1000BlackGirlBooks campaign in 2015, with the goal of amplifying diverse voices and narratives in literature.

#1000BlackGirlBooks Campaign

The #1000BlackGirlBooks campaign quickly gained momentum and captured the attention of people around the world who were inspired by Marley's vision and determination. Through social media, interviews, and public appearances, Marley raised awareness about the importance of representation in children's literature and called on individuals, organizations, and publishers to take action to address the lack of diversity in the publishing industry.

As donations poured in from across the globe, Marley exceeded her initial goal of collecting 1,000 books featuring black girls as the main characters. The books collected through the #1000BlackGirlBooks campaign were donated to schools, libraries, and community organizations in underserved communities, where they had a profound impact on readers of all ages, inspiring a new generation of young readers and storytellers.

Impact and Recognition

Marley Dias's #1000BlackGirlBooks campaign had a transformative impact on the publishing industry and sparked a broader conversation about representation, diversity, and inclusivity in children's literature. By elevating the voices of black girls and other underrepresented groups, Marley challenged the status quo and inspired publishers to take meaningful steps towards diversifying their offerings and amplifying diverse voices and perspectives.

In recognition of her advocacy work, Marley has received numerous awards and accolades, including being named to Forbes' "30 Under 30" list and Time magazine's list of the "25 Most Influential Teens of 2018." She has also been featured in media outlets such as The New York Times, NPR, and Teen Vogue, where she continues to advocate for diversity, representation, and social justice.

Ongoing Advocacy Work

Since the success of the #1000BlackGirlBooks campaign, Marley Dias has continued to be a powerful advocate for diversity and representation in children's literature. Through her platform as an author, speaker, and media personality, Marley works to amplify the voices of marginalized communities and advocate for systemic change in the publishing industry.

In 2018, Marley published her debut book, "Marley Dias Gets It Done: And So Can You!", which encourages young people to use their voices and take action to create positive change in their communities. The book became a bestseller and further solidified Marley's reputation as a leading voice for social justice and youth activism.

In addition to her writing and advocacy work, Marley is also the founder of #1000BlackGirlBooks, LLC, a social enterprise dedicated to promoting diversity and inclusion in children's literature through consulting, workshops, and events. Through her company, Marley continues to work with educators, parents, and publishers to develop resources and strategies for creating more inclusive and representative books for young readers.

Legacy and Inspiration

Marley Dias's legacy as an activist, author, and entrepreneur is profound and far-reaching. Through her #1000BlackGirlBooks campaign and ongoing advocacy work, she has inspired a generation of young people to challenge the status quo, amplify their voices, and advocate for change in their communities and the world.

Marley's impact extends beyond the publishing industry, influencing conversations and initiatives related to diversity, representation, and social justice in various fields. Her courage, determination, and unwavering commitment to her beliefs serve as a powerful example for young people everywhere, demonstrating the power of one individual to make a difference and create lasting change.

Conclusion

In conclusion, Marley Dias's journey from a passionate young reader to a leading advocate for diversity and representation in children's literature is a testament to the power of activism, storytelling, and community organizing. Through her #1000BlackGirlBooks campaign and ongoing advocacy work, she has transformed the publishing industry and inspired a new generation of readers, writers, and activists to demand more inclusive and representative stories.

Marley's legacy will endure as a beacon of hope and inspiration for generations to come, reminding us of the importance of amplifying diverse voices and narratives and creating a more inclusive and equitable world for all. As she continues her work to promote diversity and representation in children's literature and beyond, Marley Dias remains a force for positive change and a champion of social justice and equality.

Chapter 32: Autumn Peltier

Autumn Peltier, a young Indigenous activist from Canada, has emerged as a prominent voice in the global movement for clean water and environmental justice. Born on September 27, 2004, in the Wiikwemkoong Unceded Territory on Manitoulin Island in Ontario, Canada, Autumn belongs to the Wiikwemkoong First Nation, an Anishinaabe community. From a young age, she has been deeply committed to protecting water sources and advocating for Indigenous rights, drawing inspiration from her cultural heritage and the teachings of her elders. In this detailed exploration, we will delve into Autumn Peltier's background, her journey as an environmental activist, her advocacy for clean water and Indigenous rights, her impact on the global stage, and her ongoing efforts to protect water sources and promote environmental stewardship.

Early Life and Inspiration

Autumn Peltier was born into a family with a long-standing tradition of environmental stewardship and activism. Growing up in the Wiikwemkoong Unceded Territory, she was raised with a deep reverence for the natural world and a profound respect for the sacredness of water, which plays a central role in Indigenous culture and spirituality. From a young age, Autumn was taught by her elders about the importance of protecting water sources and preserving the environment for future generations.

Autumn's passion for environmental activism was ignited at the age of eight when she attended a water ceremony led by her great-aunt, Josephine Mandamin, a renowned water protector and activist. Inspired by her great-aunt's dedication to protecting water sources and her own experiences witnessing the effects of water pollution and contamination in Indigenous communities, Autumn was motivated to take action and become a voice for change.

Rise as an Environmental Activist

Autumn Peltier's journey as an environmental activist began in earnest when she attended the Children's Climate Conference in Sweden in 2015, where she delivered a powerful speech calling for action to protect water sources and address environmental degradation. Her speech, delivered to an audience of world leaders and activists, brought attention to the urgent need to safeguard water sources and respect Indigenous rights.

Since then, Autumn has become a leading voice in the global movement for clean water and environmental justice, speaking at international forums, conferences, and events to raise awareness about the impacts of water pollution and contamination on Indigenous communities. She has also been actively involved in advocating for Indigenous rights and sovereignty, calling for the recognition of Indigenous knowledge and the inclusion of Indigenous voices in decision-making processes related to environmental conservation and resource management.

Advocacy for Clean Water and Indigenous Rights

At the heart of Autumn Peltier's activism is her unwavering commitment to protecting water sources and promoting environmental justice, particularly in Indigenous communities. She has been a vocal advocate for clean water, drawing attention to the disproportionate impact of water pollution and contamination on Indigenous peoples, who often face systemic barriers to accessing safe and clean drinking water.

One of Autumn's most significant achievements as an activist came in 2016 when she addressed the United Nations General Assembly on the issue of water protection and Indigenous rights. At just 12 years old, she delivered a powerful speech urging world leaders to take action to safeguard water sources and uphold Indigenous rights, earning widespread praise and recognition for her courage and eloquence.

Since her speech at the United Nations, Autumn has continued to advocate for clean water and Indigenous rights through various channels, including public speaking engagements, media interviews, and grassroots organizing. She has used her platform to amplify the voices of Indigenous communities and call for meaningful action to address the root causes of water insecurity and environmental injustice.

Impact on the Global Stage

Autumn Peltier's advocacy efforts have had a significant impact on the global stage, bringing attention to the critical issue of water protection and Indigenous rights and inspiring people around the world to take action. Her speeches and presentations have resonated with audiences of all ages, drawing attention to the interconnectedness of environmental issues and the importance of protecting water sources for future generations.

Autumn's activism has also earned her recognition and accolades from various organizations and institutions. In 2019, she was appointed as the Chief Water Commissioner for the Anishinabek Nation, a role that allows her to advocate for water protection and Indigenous rights on a regional level. She has also received numerous awards and honors for her advocacy work, including being nominated for the International Children's Peace Prize and being named to the BBC's list of 100 inspiring and influential women of 2020.

Ongoing Efforts and Future Plans

Despite her many achievements, Autumn Peltier remains committed to her mission of protecting water sources and promoting environmental justice. She continues to advocate for clean water and Indigenous rights through her work with the Anishinabek Nation and her involvement in various grassroots initiatives and campaigns. She also plans to continue her education and pursue a career in environmental science, with the goal of contributing to efforts to address climate change and protect the environment.

Looking ahead, Autumn hopes to inspire other young people to become advocates for change and take action to address pressing environmental issues. She believes that everyone has a role to play in protecting the planet and ensuring a sustainable future for all, and she remains dedicated to amplifying Indigenous voices and promoting respect for the natural world.

Conclusion

In conclusion, Autumn Peltier's journey as an environmental activist exemplifies the power of youth leadership and Indigenous wisdom in the fight for environmental justice. Through her advocacy work, she has raised awareness about the critical importance of protecting water sources and upholding Indigenous rights, inspiring people around the world to take action to address pressing environmental challenges.

Autumn's courage, resilience, and unwavering commitment to her cause serve as a powerful example for young people everywhere, demonstrating the potential of youth activism to drive meaningful change and create a more just and sustainable world. As she continues her journey as an advocate for clean water and Indigenous rights, Autumn Peltier remains a beacon of hope and inspiration for future generations of environmental activists and changemakers.

Chapter 33: Ryan Hreljac

Ryan Hreljac is a Canadian philanthropist who gained international recognition for his remarkable initiative to provide clean and safe drinking water to communities in need around the world. Born on May 31, 1991, in Kemptville, Ontario, Canada, Ryan embarked on his mission to address the global water crisis at the tender age of six. Through his relentless determination, passion, and commitment to making a difference, Ryan has inspired millions of people and transformed countless lives through his organization, Ryan's Well Foundation. In this comprehensive exploration, we will delve into Ryan Hreljac's background, the inception of Ryan's Well Foundation, his impact on global water accessibility, the challenges he faced, and the enduring legacy of his humanitarian efforts.

Early Life and Inspiration

Ryan Hreljac's journey as a philanthropist began with a simple yet profound realization: that access to clean water is a fundamental human right that should be available to everyone, regardless of where they live. At the age of six, Ryan learned about the global water crisis from his elementary school teacher, who explained that millions of people around the world lacked access to clean and safe drinking water, leading to preventable diseases and deaths.

Inspired by what he had learned, Ryan approached his parents with a heartfelt request: to help him raise money to build a well in a community in Africa that lacked access to clean water. With his parents' support and encouragement, Ryan began doing chores around the house and asking friends and family for donations to support his cause. His determination and passion for helping others quickly captured the hearts of those around him, and before long, he had raised enough money to fund the construction of a well in Uganda.

Inception of Ryan's Well Foundation

In 1999, at the age of seven, Ryan Hreljac's dream became a reality when the first well-funded by his efforts was completed in Angolo, Uganda. The well, which provided clean and safe drinking water to hundreds of people in the community, marked the beginning of Ryan's journey as a philanthropist and the founding of Ryan's Well Foundation.

Ryan's Well Foundation is a non-profit organization dedicated to providing clean water, sanitation, and hygiene education to communities in need around the world. Since its inception, the foundation has funded over 1,400 water projects in more than 16 countries, benefiting millions of people and transforming lives through access to clean water and improved sanitation facilities.

Impact on Global Water Accessibility

Ryan Hreljac's efforts to address the global water crisis through Ryan's Well Foundation have had a profound impact on water accessibility and public health in communities around the world. By funding the construction of wells, boreholes, and water purification systems, the foundation has helped to provide clean and safe drinking water to communities that previously lacked access to this basic necessity.

Access to clean water is essential for maintaining good health, preventing waterborne diseases, and promoting economic development. By providing communities with access to clean water, Ryan's Well Foundation has not only improved public health outcomes but also empowered individuals and communities to thrive and prosper.

Challenges and Triumphs

Despite the remarkable success of Ryan's Well Foundation, Ryan Hreljac has faced numerous challenges along the way. Building wells and water projects in remote and underserved communities comes with its own set of logistical, financial, and cultural challenges, including navigating bureaucratic red tape, securing funding, and ensuring community buy-in and participation.

However, Ryan's unwavering determination and resilience have enabled him to overcome these challenges and continue his mission to provide clean water to communities in need. His ability to mobilize support, build partnerships, and inspire others to join his cause has been instrumental in the success of Ryan's Well Foundation and its impact on global water accessibility.

Recognition and Awards

Ryan Hreljac's humanitarian efforts have earned him widespread recognition and numerous awards and accolades. In 2004, he was awarded the prestigious Order of Ontario, one of the highest honors bestowed by the province of Ontario, in recognition of his outstanding contributions to addressing the global water crisis. He has also been honored with awards such as the International Children's Peace Prize and the Top 20 Under 20 Award, which recognize young people who are making a positive impact on their communities and the world.

In addition to formal recognition, Ryan's story has been featured in books, documentaries, and media outlets around the world, bringing attention to the global water crisis and inspiring others to take action to address this pressing issue.

Enduring Legacy

Ryan Hreljac's legacy as a philanthropist and humanitarian is profound and far-reaching. Through his tireless efforts to provide clean water to communities in need, he has made a tangible difference in the lives of millions of people around the world, improving public health outcomes, promoting economic development, and empowering individuals and communities to thrive.

Beyond his tangible impact, Ryan's story serves as a powerful reminder of the potential of one individual to make a difference and create positive change in the world. His humility, compassion, and unwavering commitment to his cause inspire others to take action and work towards a more just, equitable, and sustainable future for all.

Conclusion

In conclusion, Ryan Hreljac's journey from a young boy with a simple idea to a globally recognized humanitarian and philanthropist is a testament to the power of compassion, determination, and perseverance. Through his organization, Ryan's Well Foundation, he has transformed the lives of millions of people by providing access to clean water and promoting public health, economic development, and human dignity.

As Ryan's Well Foundation continues its work to address the global water crisis, Ryan Hreljac's legacy will endure as a beacon of hope and inspiration for future generations of changemakers and humanitarians. His story reminds us of the profound impact that one individual can have on the world and serves as a powerful reminder of the importance of compassion, empathy, and solidarity in creating a more just and equitable society.

Chapter 34: Greta Thunberg

Greta Thunberg is a Swedish environmental activist who rose to global prominence for her impassioned advocacy for urgent action to combat climate change. Born on January 3, 2003, in Stockholm, Sweden, Greta first gained international attention in August 2018 when, at the age of 15, she started skipping school to protest outside the Swedish Parliament, demanding stronger action from politicians to address the climate crisis. Since then, Greta has become a leading voice in the global climate movement, inspiring millions of young people around the world to join her in demanding urgent and ambitious climate action from world leaders and policymakers. In this comprehensive exploration, we will delve into Greta Thunberg's background, her journey as an environmental activist, her impact on the global stage, her activism methods, criticisms, and her ongoing efforts to raise awareness about the climate crisis and advocate for systemic change.

Early Life and Inspiration

Greta Thunberg was born into a family with a strong commitment to environmentalism and social justice. Her mother, Malena Ernman, is a well-known opera singer and environmental activist, while her father, Svante Thunberg, is an actor and author. Greta's interest in environmental issues began at a young age, fueled by discussions at home about climate change and its potential consequences for future generations.

Greta's journey as an environmental activist began in earnest when she was just 8 years old and learned about climate change in school. Deeply troubled by the scale of the crisis and the lack of action from politicians and world leaders, Greta became increasingly frustrated and disillusioned with the status quo. She struggled to understand why more wasn't being done to address what she saw as the greatest threat facing humanity.

The Birth of Fridays for Future

In August 2018, at the age of 15, Greta Thunberg decided to take matters into her own hands. Frustrated by the lack of action on climate change, she started skipping school on Fridays to protest outside the Swedish Parliament, holding a sign that read "Skolstrejk för klimatet" (School Strike for Climate). Greta's solo protest quickly gained attention from passersby, the media, and fellow activists, sparking a movement that would eventually become known as Fridays for Future.

Inspired by Greta's example, young people around the world began organizing their own school strikes and climate protests, demanding urgent action to address the climate crisis. What began as a single act of protest by a determined teenager grew into a global movement, with millions of students participating in strikes, marches, and demonstrations in cities and towns around the world.

Impact on the Global Stage

Greta Thunberg's impassioned advocacy for climate action has had a profound impact on the global stage, bringing renewed attention to the urgency of addressing the climate crisis and galvanizing support for climate action. Through her speeches, interviews, and public appearances, Greta has captured the world's attention and inspired millions of people to join the fight against climate change.

Greta's activism has also sparked a broader conversation about the role of young people in shaping the future of the planet and holding those in power accountable for their actions. By speaking truth to power and demanding action from politicians and world leaders, Greta has demonstrated the power of youth activism to drive meaningful change and shape the course of history.

Method of Activism

Greta Thunberg's method of activism is characterized by its simplicity, clarity, and unwavering commitment to her cause. At the heart of her activism is the belief that urgent and ambitious action is needed to address the climate crisis, and that politicians and world leaders must listen to the voices of young people and take their concerns seriously.

Greta's Fridays for Future protests are deliberately simple and straightforward, with her often sitting alone outside government buildings or parliament houses with a handmade sign. Her refusal to engage in traditional forms of political activism, such as lobbying or negotiation, sets her apart from other environmental activists and sends a powerful message about the need for radical change.

Criticisms and Controversies

Despite her widespread popularity and acclaim, Greta Thunberg has faced criticism and controversy from some quarters. Critics have questioned her motives, her credibility as a spokesperson for the climate movement, and the effectiveness of her activism methods. Some have accused her of being manipulated by adults or of exploiting her platform for personal gain.

Greta has also faced personal attacks and harassment from climate change deniers and online trolls, who have targeted her with abusive messages and conspiracy theories. However, she has remained resolute in the face of criticism, refusing to be deterred from her mission to raise awareness about the climate crisis and demand action from world leaders.

Greta's Speeches and Public Statements

One of the hallmarks of Greta Thunberg's activism is her powerful speeches and public statements, in which she delivers impassioned pleas for urgent action to address the climate crisis. Greta's speeches are characterized by their blunt honesty, moral clarity, and fierce determination to hold those in power accountable for their inaction.

Greta's most famous speech to date came at the United Nations Climate Action Summit in New York City in September 2019, where she delivered a scathing rebuke to world leaders for their failure to take meaningful action on climate change. In her speech, Greta condemned politicians for prioritizing economic growth over environmental sustainability and accused them of betraying future generations by ignoring the science of climate change.

Awards and Recognition

Greta Thunberg's activism has earned her widespread recognition and numerous awards and accolades. In 2019, she was named Time magazine's "Person of the Year" in recognition of her role in galvanizing the global climate movement and inspiring millions of young people to take action. She has also been honored with awards such as the Amnesty International Ambassador of Conscience Award and the Right Livelihood Award, which recognize her extraordinary contributions to human rights and environmentalism.

Ongoing Efforts and Future Plans

Despite the challenges and controversies she has faced, Greta Thunberg remains committed to her mission of raising awareness about the climate crisis and advocating for urgent action to address it. She continues to participate in climate protests, speak at international conferences and events, and engage with policymakers and world leaders to push for systemic change.

Looking ahead, Greta plans to continue her activism and use her platform to amplify the voices of young people and marginalized communities who are most affected by the impacts of climate change. She also hopes to inspire others to join the climate movement and work towards a more sustainable and equitable future for all.

Conclusion

In conclusion, Greta Thunberg's journey from a lone protester outside the Swedish Parliament to a global icon of the climate movement is a testament to the power of youth activism and the importance of speaking truth to power. Through her unwavering commitment to her cause, her impassioned speeches, and her relentless determination to hold politicians and world leaders accountable for their actions, Greta has inspired millions of people around the world to join her in demanding urgent and ambitious action to address the climate crisis.

As she continues her activism and advocacy work, Greta Thunberg remains a beacon of hope and inspiration for future generations of environmental activists and changemakers. Her courage, resilience, and unwavering commitment to her cause serve as a powerful reminder of the potential of young people to drive meaningful change and shape the course of history.

Chapter 35: Yash Gupta

Yash Gupta is a remarkable young entrepreneur and philanthropist who has gained widespread recognition for his innovative approach to addressing social and environmental challenges. Born on March 26, 1999, in Irvine, California, Yash embarked on his entrepreneurial journey at a young age, founding a successful eyewear company while still in high school. Since then, he has become a leading voice in the fields of social entrepreneurship and sustainable business, using his platform to advocate for positive change and inspire others to make a difference in their communities and the world. In this comprehensive exploration, we will delve into Yash Gupta's background, his journey as an entrepreneur and philanthropist, his innovative approach to social impact, his impact on the business world, and his ongoing efforts to create a more sustainable and equitable future.

Early Life and Inspiration

Yash Gupta's journey as an entrepreneur and philanthropist began in his early teens, inspired by his own experiences and a desire to make a positive impact in the world. Growing up in Southern California, Yash was exposed to the stark inequalities and social challenges facing many communities, including access to education and healthcare. These experiences sparked a deep sense of empathy and a determination to use his skills and resources to create positive change.

Yash's passion for entrepreneurship and social impact was also influenced by his family background and upbringing. Raised by parents who instilled in him the values of hard work, integrity, and compassion, Yash was encouraged to pursue his passions and make a difference in the world from a young age. These early influences laid the foundation for Yash's future endeavors and inspired him to chart his own path as a changemaker and innovator.

Founding of Sight Learning

At the age of 14, Yash Gupta founded Sight Learning, a socially conscious eyewear company with a mission to provide glasses to children in need around the world. The idea for Sight Learning was born out of Yash's own experience of losing his own eyeglasses while playing sports and realizing the profound impact that access to vision correction could have on a person's life.

Driven by a desire to address the global vision crisis and improve educational outcomes for underserved communities, Yash set out to create a business model that would provide affordable eyewear to those in need while also supporting sustainable development initiatives. Through Sight Learning, Yash partnered with non-profit organizations and eyewear manufacturers to distribute glasses to children in countries such as India, Nepal, and Ghana, enabling them to see clearly and pursue their education with confidence.

Impact on Education and Public Health

Sight Learning quickly gained traction and recognition for its innovative approach to addressing social and environmental challenges. By providing glasses to children in need, Yash Gupta's company not only improved educational outcomes but also promoted public health and economic development in underserved communities.

Access to vision correction is essential for children to succeed in school and achieve their full potential. Studies have shown that uncorrected vision problems can have a significant impact on academic performance and cognitive development, leading to lower grades, decreased motivation, and increased dropout rates. By providing glasses to children who need them, Sight Learning helped to remove barriers to learning and ensure that every child has the opportunity to thrive.

In addition to its impact on education, Sight Learning also contributed to improved public health outcomes by addressing the global vision crisis. Uncorrected vision problems are a leading cause of preventable blindness and visual impairment worldwide, affecting millions of people, particularly in low- and middle-income countries. By providing access to affordable eyewear, Sight Learning helped to reduce the burden of uncorrected vision problems and improve the quality of life for individuals and communities around the world.

Recognition and Awards

Yash Gupta's innovative approach to social entrepreneurship and sustainable business has earned him widespread recognition and numerous awards and accolades. In 2015, he was named one of Forbes' "30 Under 30" in the Social Entrepreneurs category, recognizing his leadership and impact in the field of social entrepreneurship. He has also been honored with awards such as the Thiel Fellowship, which provides support and funding to young entrepreneurs pursuing innovative projects with the potential for social impact.

In addition to formal recognition, Yash's work with Sight Learning has been featured in media outlets such as The New York Times, Forbes, and CNN, bringing attention to the global vision crisis and the importance of addressing social and environmental challenges through entrepreneurship and innovation.

Ongoing Efforts and Future Plans

Despite the success of Sight Learning, Yash Gupta remains committed to his mission of creating positive social and environmental impact through entrepreneurship and innovation. In recent years, he has expanded his focus to include other areas of social impact, such as sustainable development, renewable energy, and climate change mitigation.

Yash's current projects and initiatives reflect his commitment to addressing some of the most pressing challenges facing humanity and the planet. From launching sustainable energy startups to investing in renewable energy projects, Yash is leveraging his skills, resources, and network to drive positive change and create a more sustainable and equitable future for all.

Looking ahead, Yash plans to continue his work as a social entrepreneur and philanthropist, using his platform to inspire others to pursue their passions and make a difference in their communities and the world. Whether through launching new ventures, supporting social impact initiatives, or advocating for policy change, Yash remains dedicated to creating positive change and leaving a lasting legacy of impact and innovation.

Conclusion

In conclusion, Yash Gupta's journey as an entrepreneur and philanthropist exemplifies the power of entrepreneurship and innovation to create positive social and environmental impact. Through his company, Sight Learning, Yash has demonstrated the potential of business to address some of the world's most pressing challenges, from education and public health to sustainable development and renewable energy.

As he continues his journey as a changemaker and innovator, Yash Gupta remains a source of inspiration and hope for future generations of entrepreneurs, activists, and leaders. His commitment to social and environmental impact, coupled with his entrepreneurial spirit and passion for making a difference, serves as a powerful reminder of the potential of individuals to create positive change and build a better world for all.

Chapter 36: Om Prakash Yadav

Om Prakash Yadav, also known as O.P. Yadav, is an Indian politician who has played a significant role in the political landscape of Bihar, India. Born on February 5, 1973, in a small village in the Siwan district of Bihar, Yadav's journey from humble beginnings to political prominence exemplifies the complexities and dynamics of Indian politics, particularly in the state of Bihar, known for its intricate caste equations and socio-political challenges. In this comprehensive exploration, we will delve into Om Prakash Yadav's background, his rise in politics, his contributions to Bihar's political arena, his impact on society, and the challenges he has faced during his political career.

Early Life and Background

Om Prakash Yadav was born into a family with a modest background in rural Bihar. Growing up in a village with limited access to basic amenities and opportunities, Yadav experienced firsthand the socio-economic challenges faced by many people in the region. Despite the hardships, Yadav was determined to overcome his circumstances and create a better future for himself and his community.

Yadav's interest in politics and social issues was sparked at a young age, influenced by the socio-political environment of Bihar and the struggles of his own community. Inspired by leaders who championed the cause of social justice and empowerment, Yadav resolved to enter politics as a means of bringing about positive change and addressing the needs and aspirations of marginalized communities.

Entry into Politics

Om Prakash Yadav's entry into politics was a gradual process, shaped by his experiences and interactions with various political leaders and organizations in Bihar. Yadav started his political career by joining a local political party and actively participating in grassroots activities and community organizing efforts. His dedication and commitment to serving the people earned him recognition and support from the local community, paving the way for his ascent in the political hierarchy.

Over the years, Yadav emerged as a prominent leader within his party, known for his oratory skills, grassroots connect, and advocacy for the rights of marginalized communities, particularly those belonging to backward castes and economically disadvantaged backgrounds. Yadav's rise in politics was marked by his ability to mobilize support and build alliances across caste and religious lines, positioning himself as a voice of the marginalized and a champion of social justice.

Contributions to Bihar's Political Landscape

Om Prakash Yadav's contributions to Bihar's political landscape have been multifaceted, spanning various domains including governance, social welfare, and community development. As a political leader representing his constituency, Yadav has worked tirelessly to address the socio-economic challenges facing his constituents and improve their quality of life.

Yadav has been actively involved in advocating for policies and initiatives aimed at promoting inclusive growth, empowering marginalized communities, and bridging the gap between the haves and the have-nots. His efforts have focused on issues such as education, healthcare, infrastructure development, and employment generation, with a particular emphasis on uplifting the most vulnerable sections of society.

Yadav's role in Bihar's political landscape has also extended beyond his constituency, as he has been actively engaged in state-level politics and party affairs. He has served in various leadership positions within his party, contributing to the formulation of party policies and strategies, as well as representing the interests of his constituents at the state level.

Impact on Society

Om Prakash Yadav's impact on society extends beyond his political career, encompassing his efforts to bring about positive change and empower marginalized communities through social and philanthropic initiatives. Yadav has been actively involved in promoting education, healthcare, and social welfare programs, with a focus on reaching underserved and marginalized populations.

Yadav's initiatives have included the establishment of schools, hospitals, and community centers in rural areas, providing essential services and opportunities to those who need them the most. He has also been a strong advocate for women's empowerment, supporting initiatives aimed at promoting gender equality, education for girls, and economic empowerment for women.

Yadav's philanthropic endeavors have earned him respect and admiration from people across the political spectrum, as well as recognition from civil society organizations and the wider community. His commitment to serving the people and making a positive difference in their lives has made him a beloved figure among his constituents and a role model for aspiring leaders.

Challenges Faced

Om Prakash Yadav's political journey has not been without its challenges and obstacles. Bihar's political landscape is notoriously competitive and often fraught with complexities, including caste politics, criminalization, and corruption. Yadav has had to navigate these challenges while staying true to his principles and maintaining his commitment to serving the people.

Yadav has faced opposition and criticism from rival political parties and vested interests, who have sought to undermine his influence and disrupt his political career. He has also had to contend with internal challenges within his own party, including factionalism and power struggles, which have at times threatened to derail his political ambitions.

Despite these challenges, Yadav has remained resilient and steadfast in his pursuit of social and political change. His ability to connect with people, build alliances, and mobilize support has helped him overcome obstacles and emerge stronger from adversity, cementing his position as a key player in Bihar's political landscape.

Future Outlook

As Om Prakash Yadav continues his political journey, his future outlook is characterized by optimism and determination to build a better future for Bihar and its people. Yadav remains committed to his vision of inclusive and equitable development, grounded in the principles of social justice, empowerment, and good governance.

Yadav's priorities for the future include strengthening grassroots democracy, promoting transparency and accountability in governance, and fostering economic growth and social progress. He also aims to continue his efforts to empower marginalized communities, uplift the downtrodden, and bridge the gap between urban and rural areas.

In conclusion, Om Prakash Yadav's journey as a political leader exemplifies the power of perseverance, dedication, and commitment to public service. From humble beginnings to political prominence, Yadav has emerged as a champion of the marginalized and a voice for the voiceless, advocating for social justice and inclusive development in Bihar and beyond. As he continues his journey, Yadav's impact on Bihar's political landscape and society at large is sure to endure, leaving a lasting legacy of positive change and progress.

Chapter 37: Roberto Díaz Sibaja

Roberto Díaz Sibaja is a prominent figure in the realm of Costa Rican politics and public administration. Born on August 14, 1967, in San José, Costa Rica, Díaz Sibaja has dedicated his career to serving his country through various roles in government, diplomacy, and academia. His contributions to Costa Rican politics and public service have earned him respect and recognition both domestically and internationally. In this comprehensive exploration, we will delve into Roberto Díaz Sibaja's background, his career trajectory, his accomplishments, and his impact on Costa Rican society and politics.

Early Life and Education

Roberto Díaz Sibaja was born into a family with a strong tradition of public service and a deep commitment to social justice and democracy. Raised in San José, the capital city of Costa Rica, Díaz Sibaja was exposed to the vibrant political culture and democratic values that have long characterized Costa Rican society. From a young age, he was inspired by the principles of equality, justice, and solidarity, instilled in him by his family and community.

Díaz Sibaja's academic journey began at the University of Costa Rica, where he pursued a degree in law and political science. During his time at university, he distinguished himself as a diligent student with a keen intellect and a passion for public service. He was actively involved in student politics and social activism, advocating for issues such as human rights, environmental conservation, and social welfare.

Career in Government and Diplomacy

After completing his education, Roberto Díaz Sibaja embarked on a distinguished career in government and diplomacy, serving in various capacities within the Costa Rican government and representing his country on the international stage. His early years in public service were marked by his dedication to promoting democracy, human rights, and sustainable development, both at home and abroad.

Díaz Sibaja's first foray into government came in the form of a position in the Ministry of Foreign Affairs, where he worked on issues related to international cooperation and diplomacy. His diplomatic skills and expertise in international affairs soon caught the attention of senior government officials, leading to his appointment to key diplomatic posts in Costa Rican embassies and missions overseas.

As a diplomat, Díaz Sibaja played a pivotal role in representing Costa Rica's interests on a wide range of issues, including trade, security, and environmental protection. He was involved in negotiations with foreign governments and international organizations, advocating for policies and initiatives that would benefit Costa Rica and its people. His diplomatic efforts helped to strengthen Costa Rica's standing in the international community and enhance its reputation as a leader in areas such as environmental conservation and human rights.

Contributions to Public Administration

In addition to his work in diplomacy, Roberto Díaz Sibaja has made significant contributions to public administration and governance in Costa Rica. He has held several high-level positions within the Costa Rican government, where he has been instrumental in shaping public policy and implementing reforms aimed at improving the lives of Costa Ricans.

One of Díaz Sibaja's most notable roles in public administration was his appointment as Minister of Public Security, where he oversaw efforts to combat crime, strengthen law enforcement, and promote citizen safety. During his tenure, he implemented a series of reforms aimed at modernizing Costa Rica's police force, improving coordination among law enforcement agencies, and enhancing public trust in the justice system.

Díaz Sibaja's leadership in public security earned him praise for his commitment to tackling the root causes of crime and violence, including poverty, inequality, and social exclusion. He worked closely with civil society organizations, community leaders, and international partners to develop comprehensive strategies for crime prevention and youth empowerment, emphasizing the importance of addressing the underlying socio-economic factors that contribute to crime.

Advocacy for Sustainable Development

Throughout his career, Roberto Díaz Sibaja has been a passionate advocate for sustainable development and environmental conservation. He has been actively involved in efforts to protect Costa Rica's natural resources, preserve its biodiversity, and promote sustainable practices in areas such as agriculture, tourism, and energy.

Díaz Sibaja's advocacy for sustainable development is rooted in Costa Rica's rich environmental heritage and its longstanding commitment to conservation. He has been a vocal proponent of policies and initiatives aimed at promoting renewable energy, reducing carbon emissions, and mitigating the impacts of climate change. His efforts have helped to position Costa Rica as a global leader in environmental sustainability and green development.

International Recognition and Awards

Roberto Díaz Sibaja's contributions to Costa Rican politics and public service have earned him recognition and accolades both domestically and internationally. He has been honored with awards and honors from governments, organizations, and institutions around the world, in recognition of his leadership, integrity, and dedication to public service.

Díaz Sibaja's diplomatic achievements have been recognized by foreign governments and international organizations, who have praised his efforts to promote peace, security, and cooperation on the world stage. He has been awarded medals of honor, honorary citizenships, and other prestigious awards for his contributions to international diplomacy and global governance.

Legacy and Impact

Roberto Díaz Sibaja's legacy as a statesman, diplomat, and public servant is characterized by his unwavering commitment to serving the people of Costa Rica and promoting the values of democracy, human rights, and sustainable development. Throughout his career, he has demonstrated exemplary leadership, integrity, and dedication to the public good, earning the respect and admiration of his colleagues, peers, and constituents.

Díaz Sibaja's impact on Costa Rican society and politics is far-reaching, encompassing his contributions to governance, diplomacy, and environmental conservation. His efforts have helped to shape the course of Costa Rican history and establish the country as a beacon of democracy and progress in the region and beyond.

As he continues his journey in public service, Roberto Díaz Sibaja remains committed to his mission of building a better future for Costa Rica and its people. His leadership and vision will continue to inspire future generations of leaders and serve as a guiding light for those who seek to make a positive difference in the world.

Chapter 38: Katie Stagliano

Katie Stagliano, a name synonymous with generosity, compassion, and innovation, has become a symbol of hope and inspiration for countless individuals around the world. Born on January 28, 2000, in Summerville, South Carolina, Katie's remarkable journey began at a young age when she embarked on a mission to combat hunger and food insecurity in her community. Through her innovative gardening project, Katie has not only transformed barren land into flourishing gardens but has also cultivated a sense of community, empathy, and empowerment among those she serves. In this comprehensive exploration, we will delve into Katie Stagliano's background, her founding of the Katie's Krops initiative, her impact on hunger relief efforts, her recognition and awards, and her ongoing dedication to making a difference in the lives of others.

Early Life and Inspiration

Katie Stagliano's journey as a changemaker and philanthropist began at the tender age of nine when she received a cabbage seedling as part of a school gardening project. Little did she know that this seemingly ordinary seedling would plant the seeds of inspiration that would blossom into a movement to combat hunger and food insecurity in her community.

As Katie tended to her cabbage plant, she was struck by its rapid growth and abundance. Realizing that she had more cabbage than she could consume herself, Katie decided to donate it to a local soup kitchen to help feed those in need. This simple act of kindness sparked a fire within Katie, igniting her passion for helping others and setting her on a path of service and activism that would define her life's work.

Founding of Katie's Krops

Inspired by her experience with the cabbage plant and driven by a desire to make a tangible impact on hunger in her community, Katie Stagliano founded Katie's Krops in 2008 at the age of nine. The mission of Katie's Krops is simple yet powerful: to empower youth to end hunger one vegetable garden at a time.

The premise of Katie's Krops is based on the idea that anyone, regardless of age or background, can make a difference in the fight against hunger. Through Katie's Krops, young people are provided with the resources, support, and guidance they need to plant, tend, and harvest their own vegetable gardens, with the produce being donated to local food banks, soup kitchens, and community organizations.

Growth and Expansion

Since its inception, Katie's Krops has grown exponentially, expanding its reach and impact beyond Katie's hometown of Summerville, South Carolina, to communities across the United States. Through a network of youth-led gardens, Katie's Krops has helped to feed thousands of individuals and families facing food insecurity, providing them with access to fresh, nutritious produce and promoting healthy eating habits.

The success of Katie's Krops can be attributed to Katie's vision, leadership, and unwavering commitment to her mission, as well as the dedication and enthusiasm of the young people who participate in the program. Together, they have transformed vacant lots, schoolyards, and community spaces into vibrant gardens that not only nourish the body but also feed the soul.

Impact on Hunger Relief Efforts

Katie's Krops has had a profound impact on hunger relief efforts in communities across the United States, providing much-needed support to individuals and families facing food insecurity. By empowering young people to take action and make a difference in their communities, Katie's Krops has not only helped to alleviate hunger but has also fostered a sense of empathy, compassion, and social responsibility among the next generation of leaders.

Through their efforts, Katie and the young gardeners of Katie's Krops have helped to raise awareness about the issue of hunger and the importance of addressing food insecurity at the local level. They have inspired others to get involved in hunger relief efforts, whether through volunteering, donating, or starting their own community gardens.

Recognition and Awards

Katie Stagliano's tireless efforts to combat hunger and food insecurity have not gone unnoticed. She has been honored with numerous awards and accolades for her leadership, compassion, and dedication to making a difference in the lives of others.

In 2011, Katie received the Clinton Global Citizen Award for her work with Katie's Krops, recognizing her as a young leader who has made a significant contribution to addressing global challenges. She has also been honored with the Prudential Spirit of Community Award, the Jefferson Award for Public Service, and the Gloria Barron Prize for Young Heroes, among others.

Ongoing Dedication and Future Plans

Despite her many accomplishments, Katie Stagliano remains humble and grounded, continuing to devote herself to the mission of Katie's Krops and the fight against hunger. She is actively involved in the day-to-day operations of the organization, working tirelessly to expand its reach, engage more young people, and make an even greater impact on hunger relief efforts.

Looking ahead, Katie has ambitious plans for the future of Katie's Krops, including expanding its programs and initiatives to reach more communities in need, developing educational resources and curriculum materials to support youth-led gardening projects, and advocating for policies and initiatives that address the root causes of hunger and food insecurity.

Conclusion

In conclusion, Katie Stagliano's remarkable journey from a nine-year-old girl with a cabbage seedling to a visionary leader and changemaker is a testament to the power of compassion, empathy, and determination to make a difference in the world. Through her innovative gardening project and the founding of Katie's Krops, Katie has not only helped to alleviate hunger and food insecurity in communities across the United States but has also inspired a new generation of young leaders to take action and create positive change in their communities.

As she continues her journey, Katie Stagliano remains a beacon of hope and inspiration for individuals of all ages who aspire to make a difference in the world. Her dedication to the fight against hunger and her commitment to empowering young people to take action serve as a powerful reminder of the potential we all have to create a more just, equitable, and compassionate society.

Chapter 39: Zuriel Oduwole

Zuriel Oduwole, a name that resonates with empowerment, advocacy, and inspiration, is a young African-American filmmaker, education advocate, and girls' education activist. Born on April 27, 2002, in Los Angeles, California, Zuriel's journey to becoming a global advocate for education and gender equality began at a remarkably young age. Her tireless efforts to promote education and empower girls in Africa and around the world have earned her widespread recognition and admiration. In this comprehensive exploration, we will delve into Zuriel Oduwole's background, her journey as an advocate and filmmaker, her impact on education advocacy, her recognition and awards, and her ongoing dedication to making a difference in the lives of girls and young people worldwide.

Early Life and Inspiration

Zuriel Oduwole's passion for education and advocacy was ignited at a young age, inspired by her own experiences and a desire to make a positive impact in the world. Growing up in a diverse and multicultural environment in Los Angeles, Zuriel was exposed to the importance of education and the power of knowledge from an early age. Her parents, both of Nigerian descent, instilled in her the values of hard work, perseverance, and social responsibility, encouraging her to pursue her passions and use her voice to effect change.

Zuriel's interest in filmmaking and storytelling was sparked by her love of movies and documentaries, which she watched avidly with her family. Inspired by the stories of courageous individuals who overcame adversity to achieve their dreams, Zuriel realized the potential of film as a powerful tool for advocacy and social change. She began experimenting with filmmaking at a young age, using her creativity and imagination to tell stories that would inspire and empower others.

Advocacy for Girls' Education

Zuriel Oduwole's advocacy for girls' education and gender equality has been a central focus of her work since the beginning of her journey. Recognizing the transformative power of education in unlocking opportunities and breaking the cycle of poverty, Zuriel has been a vocal advocate for ensuring that all children, regardless of their gender or background, have access to quality education.

Zuriel's advocacy efforts have focused primarily on highlighting the barriers that girls face in accessing education, particularly in developing countries, and advocating for policies and initiatives that promote gender equality in education. Through her films, speeches, and social media platforms, Zuriel has raised awareness about the importance of girls' education and the need to address issues such as child marriage, gender-based violence, and cultural barriers to girls' schooling.

Journey as a Filmmaker

Zuriel Oduwole's journey as a filmmaker began in earnest when she was just ten years old, with the release of her first documentary film, "The Education of an American Girl." The film, which explored Zuriel's own experiences as a young African-American girl growing up in America, received widespread acclaim for its honesty, authenticity, and insight into the challenges and opportunities facing girls around the world.

Building on the success of her first film, Zuriel went on to produce a series of documentaries focused on girls' education and empowerment in Africa. Her films, which have been screened at international film festivals and events, have shed light on the struggles and triumphs of girls in countries such as Nigeria, Ghana, Kenya, and Tanzania, amplifying their voices and stories on the global stage.

Impact on Education Advocacy

Zuriel Oduwole's impact on education advocacy has been significant, inspiring young people around the world to take action and make a difference in their communities. Through her films, speeches, and advocacy campaigns, Zuriel has raised awareness about the importance of education as a fundamental human right and a key driver of social and economic development.

Zuriel's advocacy efforts have led to tangible results, including increased funding for girls' education programs, policy changes to promote gender equality in education, and greater investment in teacher training and school infrastructure. Her work has also helped to challenge stereotypes and misconceptions about girls' capabilities and potential, encouraging society to rethink traditional gender roles and norms.

Recognition and Awards

Zuriel Oduwole's tireless efforts to promote education and empower girls have earned her widespread recognition and numerous awards and accolades. She has been honored with prestigious awards such as the Nelson Mandela International Peace Award, the Harriet Tubman Civil Rights Award, and the Martin Luther King Jr. Leadership Award, among others.

In addition to formal recognition, Zuriel has been featured in media outlets such as Forbes, CNN, BBC, and Time magazine, bringing attention to her work and amplifying her message of education and empowerment. She has also been invited to speak at international conferences, events, and forums, where she has shared her story and inspired audiences with her passion, eloquence, and determination.

Ongoing Dedication and Future Plans

Despite her many accomplishments, Zuriel Oduwole remains humble and grounded, continuing to devote herself to the cause of education and gender equality. She is actively involved in a variety of initiatives and projects aimed at empowering girls and promoting education as a driver of social change.

Looking ahead, Zuriel plans to expand her advocacy efforts and reach even more young people around the world. She is committed to using her platform and voice to raise awareness about the importance of education and to advocate for policies and programs that support the rights and aspirations of girls and young women.

Conclusion

In conclusion, Zuriel Oduwole's journey as an advocate, filmmaker, and education activist serves as a powerful example of the impact that one person can have on the world. From a young age, Zuriel has demonstrated courage, determination, and compassion in her efforts to promote education and empower girls, inspiring others to join her in the fight for a more just, equitable, and inclusive world.

As she continues her journey, Zuriel remains a beacon of hope and inspiration for young people everywhere, reminding us of the power of education to transform lives and communities. Her dedication, passion, and commitment to making a difference serve as a powerful reminder that no dream is too big, and no challenge is too daunting when we work together to create a better future for all.

Chapter 40: Jack Andraka

Jack Andraka, a prodigious young scientist and innovator, has captured the world's attention with his groundbreaking work in the field of cancer research. Born on January 8, 1997, in Crownsville, Maryland, Jack's journey to scientific stardom began at a remarkably young age when he developed a revolutionary new method for detecting pancreatic cancer. His remarkable achievement, which earned him numerous awards and accolades, has not only transformed the field of cancer diagnostics but has also inspired a new generation of young scientists to pursue their passions and make a difference in the world. In this comprehensive exploration, we will delve into Jack Andraka's background, his groundbreaking discovery, his impact on cancer research, his recognition and awards, and his ongoing dedication to scientific innovation and social entrepreneurship.

Early Life and Inspiration

Jack Andraka's interest in science and innovation was sparked at a young age, inspired by his curiosity about the natural world and a desire to understand how things work. Growing up in Crownsville, Maryland, Jack was surrounded by a supportive family who nurtured his passion for learning and encouraged him to pursue his interests in science and technology.

From an early age, Jack showed a keen interest in biology, chemistry, and computer science, spending countless hours conducting experiments in his makeshift home laboratory and devouring books and articles on a wide range of scientific topics. His insatiable curiosity and thirst for knowledge set him apart from his peers and laid the foundation for his future success as a scientist and innovator.

Breakthrough Discovery: The Pancreatic Cancer Test

Jack Andraka's breakthrough discovery came in 2012 when he was just 15 years old. Inspired by the tragic death of a family friend from pancreatic cancer, Jack set out to find a better way to detect the disease early, when it is most treatable. Drawing on his background in biology and chemistry, as well as his passion for innovation, Jack developed a novel method for detecting pancreatic cancer using a simple paper sensor.

The key to Jack's groundbreaking discovery was his use of carbon nanotubes, tiny structures made of carbon atoms, which have unique properties that make them highly sensitive to changes in the environment. By coating the nanotubes with antibodies that bind specifically to a protein associated with pancreatic cancer, Jack was able to create a sensor that could detect the presence of the protein in blood or urine samples, providing an early warning sign of the disease.

Jack's pancreatic cancer test is not only highly sensitive and accurate but also inexpensive and easy to use, making it potentially life-saving for millions of people around the world. His innovative approach to cancer diagnostics has the potential to revolutionize the way we detect and treat cancer, leading to earlier diagnosis, more effective treatment, and ultimately, better outcomes for patients.

Impact on Cancer Research

Jack Andraka's groundbreaking discovery has had a profound impact on cancer research and has opened up new possibilities for early detection and treatment of the disease. His pancreatic cancer test has been hailed as a game-changer in the field of oncology, offering hope to millions of people who are at risk of developing this deadly form of cancer.

In addition to his work on pancreatic cancer, Jack has also been involved in research projects focused on other types of cancer, including breast cancer, lung cancer, and ovarian cancer. His innovative approaches to cancer diagnostics and treatment have earned him recognition from leading scientists and medical professionals around the world, who have praised his creativity, ingenuity, and commitment to advancing the fight against cancer.

Recognition and Awards

Jack Andraka's remarkable achievements have earned him numerous awards and accolades, including the Intel Science Talent Search, the Gordon E. Moore Award, and the National Geographic Emerging Explorer Award, among others. He has also been recognized by prestigious institutions such as the Smithsonian Institution, the National Institutes of Health, and the United Nations, for his contributions to science and innovation.

In addition to formal recognition, Jack has been featured in media outlets such as CNN, BBC, The New York Times, and Time magazine, bringing attention to his work and amplifying his message of hope and inspiration. He has also been invited to speak at international conferences, events, and forums, where he has shared his story and inspired audiences with his passion, vision, and determination.

Ongoing Dedication and Future Plans

Despite his many accomplishments, Jack Andraka remains humble and grounded, continuing to devote himself to scientific innovation and social entrepreneurship. He is actively involved in a variety of initiatives and projects aimed at promoting STEM education, empowering young scientists, and advancing the frontiers of knowledge.

Looking ahead, Jack plans to continue his research in cancer diagnostics and treatment, with a focus on developing new technologies and approaches to improve outcomes for patients. He also aims to inspire and mentor the next generation of young scientists, encouraging them to pursue their passions and make a difference in the world.

Conclusion

In conclusion, Jack Andraka's journey from a curious teenager experimenting in his home laboratory to a globally recognized scientist and innovator is a testament to the power of passion, perseverance, and ingenuity. His groundbreaking discovery of a new method for detecting pancreatic cancer has not only transformed the field of cancer research but has also inspired a new generation of young scientists to dream big and think outside the box.

As he continues his journey, Jack Andraka remains committed to his mission of advancing scientific knowledge, improving human health, and making a positive impact on the world. His dedication, passion, and creativity serve as a powerful reminder that no challenge is too great, and no dream is too ambitious when we dare to imagine, innovate, and believe in the power of science to change lives.

Epilogue

As we close the final chapter of "Powerful Kids," we are left with a profound sense of hope and inspiration. The stories of the remarkable young individuals featured in this book remind us that age is not a barrier to making significant contributions to society. Their journeys, filled with determination, resilience, and innovation, showcase the boundless potential of youth to drive change and address some of the world's most pressing challenges.

These powerful kids come from diverse backgrounds and face unique obstacles, yet they share a common thread: an unwavering commitment to making the world a better place. Whether through scientific discovery, social activism, environmental advocacy, or creative expression, they have each found their own way to impact their communities and beyond. Their achievements are a testament to what can be accomplished when passion meets purpose, and when young voices are heard and valued.

The young leaders highlighted in this book are not just exceptional outliers; they are representatives of a broader movement. Across the globe, countless other young people are stepping up to tackle issues that matter to them, fueled by a sense of urgency and a vision for a brighter future. They are challenging norms, questioning the status quo, and pushing boundaries in ways that many adults might find daunting. Their fresh perspectives and innovative approaches are exactly what we need in a rapidly changing world.

As we reflect on the incredible stories within these pages, it becomes clear that supporting and empowering young people is not just beneficial but essential. They bring new ideas, fearless energy, and a deep sense of empathy that can rejuvenate and transform societies. It is our collective responsibility to create environments where these young changemakers can thrive. This means providing access to quality education, encouraging curiosity and critical thinking, fostering inclusivity, and ensuring that young voices are not just heard but actively listened to and acted upon.

The impact of these young leaders extends beyond their immediate achievements. They inspire peers, mentor younger generations, and remind us all of the power of youth. Their stories demonstrate that when given the tools, opportunities, and encouragement, young people can accomplish extraordinary things. They challenge us to rethink how we view youth and to recognize the incredible potential within every young person.

As we move forward, let us carry the lessons from "Powerful Kids" with us. Let us celebrate the successes of these young trailblazers and support the next wave of innovators, activists, and leaders. Let their stories inspire us to take action in our own lives, to mentor and guide the youth around us, and to advocate for systems that empower young people globally.

In closing, "Powerful Kids" is not just a compilation of remarkable stories; it is a call to action. It is a reminder that the future is in the hands of the youth, and with the right support and encouragement, they can achieve greatness. Let us be the champions who stand behind them, fostering a world where every young person can realize their full potential and contribute to a better, more just, and sustainable world.

The journey does not end here. As we turn the final page, we look to the future with optimism, ready to support and celebrate the powerful kids who will continue to shape our world in ways we cannot yet imagine. The baton of change is in their hands, and with their leadership, the future looks incredibly bright.

The End.